T0358254

Cambridge Elements ≡

Elements in Historical Theory and Practice
edited by
Daniel Woolf
Queen's University, Ontario

THE HISTORY
OF KNOWLEDGE

Johan Östling
Lund University

David Larsson Heidenblad
Lund University

(Translation by Lena Olsson)

Shaftesbury Road, Cambridge CB2 8EA, United Kingdom

One Liberty Plaza, 20th Floor, New York, NY 10006, USA

477 Williamstown Road, Port Melbourne, VIC 3207, Australia

314–321, 3rd Floor, Plot 3, Splendor Forum, Jasola District Centre,
New Delhi – 110025, India

103 Penang Road, #05–06/07, Visioncrest Commercial, Singapore 238467

Cambridge University Press is part of Cambridge University Press & Assessment,
a department of the University of Cambridge.

We share the University's mission to contribute to society through the pursuit of
education, learning and research at the highest international levels of excellence.

www.cambridge.org
Information on this title: www.cambridge.org/9781009486903

DOI: 10.1017/9781009047715

When citing this work, please include a reference to the DOI 10.1017/9781009047715

First published 2023

A catalogue record for this publication is available from the British Library

ISBN 978-1-009-48690-3 Hardback
ISBN 978-1-009-04854-5 Paperback
ISSN 2634-8616 (online)
ISSN 2634-8608 (print)

The History of Knowledge

Elements in Historical Theory and Practice

DOI: 10.1017/9781009047715
First published online: December 2023

Johan Östling
Lund University

David Larsson Heidenblad
Lund University

(Translation by Lena Olsson)

Author for correspondence: Johan Östling, johan.ostling@hist.lu.se

Abstract: This Element provides a pedagogical overview of the history of knowledge, including its main currents, distinguishing ideas, and key concepts. However, it is not primarily a state-of-the-art overview but rather an argumentative contribution that seeks to push the field in a certain direction – towards studying knowledge in society and knowledge in people's lives. Hence, the history of knowledge envisioned by the authors is not a rebranding of the history of science and intellectual history, but rather a reinvigoration of social and cultural history. This implies that many different forms of knowledge should be objects of study. By drawing on ongoing research from all across the world dealing with different time periods and problems, the authors demonstrate that the history of knowledge can enrich our understanding of past societies. This title is also available as Open Access on Cambridge Core.

Keywords: history of knowledge, knowledge, circulation of knowledge, knowledge actors, forms of knowledge

ISBNs: 9781009486903 (HB), 9781009048545 (PB), 9781009047715 (OC)
ISSNs: 2634-8616 (online), 2634-8608 (print)

Contents

1 Pathways to the History of Knowledge 1

2 Key Concepts in the History of Knowledge 16

3 Knowledge in Circulation 31

4 The Future of the History of Knowledge 56

Further Reading 59

Bibliography 63

1 Pathways to the History of Knowledge

On 9 August 1995, Netscape Communications Corporation was floated on the American NASDAQ stock exchange. The company was then only sixteen months old and did not turn a profit. But its browser – Netscape Navigator – dominated the Internet, the hottest technology of the day. The interest from the media and financial markets was enormous. When the first trading day was over, the introductory share price had more than doubled and Netscape's market value was $2.9 billion. Was this the beginning of a new era, and if so, what would it bring with it? Would the Internet disrupt our entire existence, or was it simply a fad?[1]

In the mid-1990s, questions like these were highly topical. But uncertainty was great, even in Silicon Valley. There, business executives and entrepreneurs were used to rapid technical development, big promises, and radical visions of the future. Sometimes these materialised, but often they did not. Would it be possible to navigate through this? Someone who thought long and hard about this was Andrew Grove, a long-time managing director of the market-leading semiconductor manufacturer Intel. He was there at the company's founding in 1968 and had lived through several radical changes, including Intel's shift in the mid-1980s of its production from memory chips to microprocessors.

At the time of Netscape's flotation on the stock exchange, Grove was writing a book that would eventually be titled *Only the Paranoid Survive*. Initially published in 1996, it is still in print, in spite of its examples now being obsolete. The reason the book continues to find new readers is that the principal challenge discussed by Grove remains: how should companies and individuals behave in a world that is in a constant state of flux? And above all: what should one do when the world's dynamics are upended, when new technologies, laws, competitors, or world events make that which once functioned no longer able to do so?

The final chapter in *Only the Paranoid Survive* is about the Internet. In this chapter Grove perceptively, almost prophetically, discusses the potential significance of this technology for telecom operators, software developers, retailers, and media companies. His discussion indicates that the Internet will probably rock the very foundations of many companies and businesses – but not of Intel. At the same time, his gut tells him otherwise. He realises that the interconnections of the world's computers will affect his company at a foundational level. It is high time to prepare for a different world.[2]

Retrospectively, this course of action may seem obvious. Surely, it was evident to anyone – in particular to a director at one of the leading tech

---

[1] O'Mara, *Code*. [2] Grove, *Only*.

companies of the 1990s – that the Internet would pave the way for a new world? But it is not quite that simple. It is difficult for people to appreciate the extent of changes they experience, even for actors who have real power to steer development in a particular direction. The future is always more unsure and elusive in real-time than retrospectively.

Andrew Grove can therefore hardly be blamed for not having discussed the future significance of the Internet for the conditions, effects, and forms of our shared knowledge. He was of course aware of Microsoft's attempt to create a digital encyclopaedia called *Encarta*, but he had no idea that within a decade we would all be googling online and seeking knowledge on *Wikipedia*. Smartphones, streaming services, and social media were not on the map, let alone on the horizon. A few decades further on it is, however, clear that in just a short time the foundations were profoundly shaken. This happened at a societal level, where the prerequisites for communication, the circulation of knowledge, and political mobilisation were repeatedly disrupted. But it also occurred at an individual level, where today our everyday lives in principle demand access to a mobile phone and an Internet connection. When we need to learn something new, the first step is a search engine, and the next is a freely accessible text, instruction film, or podcast. Media infrastructure, the composition of the knowledge society, and the preconditions for global knowledge work are completely different today than they were in the mid-1990s. Put briefly: the world before the Internet is now history. And we who are around after this inflection point should – as Andrew Grove did in 1996 – have the good sense to realise that the time of revolutionary change is not past. Momentous things will continue to happen, even if we cannot know what, when, how, or what consequences they will have.

But can history give us any guidance? We believe so. If nothing else, it may give us insights from other times when the basic preconditions of knowledge changed. For instance, this happened with the invention of the first written languages in ancient Mesopotamia, Egypt, India, and China. Writing permitted the transfer of knowledge between generations and different places without the direct interaction of people. It made possible civilisations, world religions, cultural specialisation, and the concentration of wealth and power. Another example is the impact of the printing press in fifteenth-century Europe. It created completely new opportunities for writing down, disseminating, storing, and using knowledge. The sixteenth-century Reformation can hardly be imagined without such technical and media changes. This is true even though social movements, protests, and power struggles – then and later – were also constructed through close relationships, the spoken word, institutions of learning, and political alliances.[3]

If we look further ahead, towards the end of the nineteenth century, we can see how modern journalism and the political party system in the Western world developed symbiotically with the spread of universal literacy. The great breakthrough occurred when cheaper production technologies and subsidised mail services had made it economically profitable to print newspapers in mass editions. Simultaneously, conflict levels increased in societies that had industrialised. Workers organised, as did employers. The struggle centred on democracy, universal suffrage, and economic distribution, but also on what the state and the authorities, the armed forces, and the educational system should be. At universities, polytechnics, and growing businesses ever greater resources were allocated to the natural sciences, technology, and medicine. At the same time, an established culture of learning with humanistic overtones remained strong, influencing art, culture, and public discussions of ideas. What was the place of knowledge between tradition and modernity, ideology and idealism?[4]

If we turn to the initial decades of the post-war era, we again see different patterns. At this time, the state and the military emerged as the major research-funding bodies. From here, there is a direct line to Andrew Grove and the Internet. Without enormous federal investments in military technology after the Sputnik Shock of 1957, Silicon Valley would never have existed. Many other wealthy nations invested a lot of money in higher education, which grew substantially. The old elite university was replaced by a more democratic mass university. In parallel with this, television, press, and radio flourished. In the United Kingdom, the BBC dominated the airwaves and became the model for public service channels in other countries. In the mid-1960s, many countries had a single or only a few TV channels whose social reach and importance are difficult to imagine today. Prosperity increased, and the vehicle-borne consumption society took shape alongside political investments in longer schooling for boys and girls, regardless of their backgrounds. The large baby boom cohorts born after the end of World War II had completely different preconditions than their parents.[5]

Historians' interest in processes like those discussed has increased during the twenty-first century. After all, historians are, like everyone else, products of their time. Those of us who have lived through the digital revolution have witnessed changes in media and knowledge systems that have increased our sensitivity for detecting similar phenomena in the past. Simple historical parallels are rarely easy to draw. But contemporary experiences enable us to notice

---

[3] Eisenstein, *Printing*.   [4] Bayly, *Birth*.   [5] Östling, *Histories*.

new processes and phenomena in the past, things to which previous generations of historians did not attach as much weight. And our historical knowledge enables us to establish comparisons in which to reflect our own time. What is similar and what is different? What changes and what does not? Is our current condition truly new and, if so, in what ways?

Questions like these are fundamental to the writers of this Element. We are two historians at Lund University in Sweden who, together with our colleagues, have endeavoured to introduce, establish, and develop a new field of research: the history of knowledge. At an early stage, we were inspired by discussions in the German-speaking part of the world. It was there, just after the turn of the millennium, that arguments emerged for replacing or complementing the traditional history of science (*Wissenschaftsgeschichte*) with a new history of knowledge (*Wissensgeschichte*). Its focus would lie on broader societal contexts rather than on institutions of learning and elite actors. A watchword of the time was *circulation*. This created associations to globalisation and the Internet, and to the movement of people, capital, knowledge, and ideas. Researchers did not uncritically embrace the concept of circulation, but they felt it could be used in order to study and analyse the past in new ways.[6]

In parallel with our initial work on the history of knowledge, the field has attracted ever greater attention in the English-speaking world. One can say that this research field entered a new and more international phase in the mid-2010s. This intensity has increased markedly over the last few years, and American, Australian, British, Dutch, and Nordic researchers have begun to make contributions that deal explicitly with the history of knowledge.[7]

What we are dealing with is, fundamentally, a shift in perspective. By making knowledge – not science, culture, politics, or ideas – central to historical study, new questions, methods, research objects, and source materials become significant. But what does this mean in practice? What is the history of knowledge, and how is it done? In this Element, we want to provide our answers, and to encourage our readers to apply their own history of knowledge perspectives on the past.

In order to accomplish this, we introduce a number of key concepts and perspectives that are fundamental for today's history of knowledge in the following sections. However, our Element is not primarily a general overview of the field. There are already several relatively recently published works of this kind by British scholar Peter Burke and German scholar Marian Füssel, both of whom are experts on early modern history.[8] What we instead do in this Element is combine a qualified introduction to the history of knowledge with an argumentative

---

[6] Sarasin, 'Was ist'.   [7] Östling, 'Developing'.   [8] Burke, *What Is*; Füssel, *Wissen*.

contribution that seeks to push the field in a certain direction. As experts on modern and contemporary history, anchored in a Scandinavian context and with a special interest in the circulation of knowledge in society, our points of departure and empirical evidence will differ somewhat from that of scholars like Burke and Füssel. We hope to provide a good introduction to the subject but also enrich the discussion on how the history of knowledge can be conducted. In this introductory section, we discuss how historians of knowledge think about knowledge, and highlight the field's main directions and sources of inspiration. In the second section, we explain key analytical concepts. In the third section, we then show, using examples taken mainly from our own research, the practical implications of investigations in the history of knowledge. In the fourth and final section, we look ahead towards the future of the field.

1.1 The Concept of Knowledge

Historians of knowledge regard knowledge as a socially and historically determined phenomenon. The focus is on what people in various societies and times have believed they know about themselves and the world. Consequently, anything perceived, dealt with, or acted on as knowledge becomes potentially interesting to study. Whether the knowledge claims of past generations are today considered well-founded or true is, as a general rule, not interesting to a historian of knowledge. What we study instead is how something became knowledge for people and what the consequences of this were for different societies and cultures.

This foundational way of looking at knowledge is something historians of knowledge share with anthropologists and sociologists. We all emphasise that knowledge is always embedded in larger cultural and social contexts. In this context, Norwegian anthropologist Fredrik Barth has spoken about traditions of knowledge as consisting of a collection of statements about the world, conveyed through words and symbols, within some kind of institutionalised social relations. Various aspects are interwoven with one another. Knowledge can thus not be something exclusively individual or particular. Instead, it is generated by people sharing and jointly maintaining it.[9]

The philosophical reflections on what knowledge is stretch back to antiquity. Plato defined knowledge as well-justified belief. But how can we know what beliefs are well-justified? For his part, Aristotle underlined that there were different forms of knowledge: *episteme* is rational or theoretical knowledge, *techne* is artisanal or artistic knowledge, and *phronesis* is practical knowledge, sagacity, or wisdom. Many historians of knowledge have favoured these

---

[9] Barth, 'Anthropology'.

distinctions, not least because they enable a broader historical study of the types of knowledge that exist and operate far beyond the worlds of learning.[10]

A complicated question is whether the truth of a knowledge claim actually matters to a historian of knowledge. Are astrology, alchemy, and astronomy equally viable objects of study? Yes, on one level they are. If it can be shown that people have treated something as knowledge, then it is fruitful to investigate it as such. Historians of knowledge do not wish to judge past systems of thought and knowledge. The history of knowledge includes various kinds of scholarship – but these are not the only, or even necessarily the primary, objects of study. At the same time, there are divisions within the field. Some researchers and scholars, including Philipp Sarasin, have argued that knowledge historians should concentrate on analysing systematic and rational forms of knowledge. He makes an enquiry into the value of seeing, for example, conspiracy theories as knowledge phenomena. Sarasin is aware, however, of the difficulties of establishing such boundaries in practice. He also maintains that knowledge-historical methods can be used to study phenomena that scholars themselves believe are irrational or superstitious.[11]

Another aspect of this problem is whether our analysis is contingent on historical actors themselves having referred to knowledge using the term *knowledge* or one of its synonyms. If so, it is only conscious knowledge that is studied. But people can be both unaware of – or stay silent about – that which they employ as knowledge, perhaps because it appears so obviously true for them that it does not need stating aloud or writing down. Or perhaps they lack the necessary analytical concepts or live in a culture where these do not exist. For this reason, Jürgen Renn feels that one should steer a middle course between knowledge as a category used by historical actors (what people have believed to be knowledge) and knowledge as a strictly analytical category (what researchers define as knowledge after the fact). The former may lead to a radically subjectivist or relativist position that makes it impossible to compare phenomena across time and space. The latter risks becoming anachronistic, awkward, and difficult to apply empirically in historical studies. Renn's way out of this dilemma is to see history of knowledge studies as explorations of both the past and of the question of what knowledge really is.[12]

What we see here is tension between the history of knowledge as a science of objects of research (where the main issue is what knowledge is and has been) and the history of knowledge as a cluster of perspectives on the past (where the value of knowledge is as an entry point which helps us investigate other things). Like Jürgen Renn, we feel that the history of knowledge should be both of these

---

[10] Östling, 'Kunskap'.   [11] Sarasin, 'More Than'.   [12] Renn, *Evolution*.

things, but we nevertheless see the shift in perspective as paramount. The most important thing about investigations in the history of knowledge is that they provide new understanding of past societies, phenomena, and processes of change. Therefore, we do not find it problematic that the history of knowledge adopts a broad, imprecise concept of knowledge.

There are, however, critics who reason differently. What is *not* knowledge? they ask. Other researchers have tried to turn this objection into a solution to the problem. Lukas Verburgt and Peter Burke feel that it is especially fruitful to focus on the boundaries of knowledge, on what is considered ignorance or what is even ignored. It is then possible to indirectly make visible and analyse what knowledge has been and how it has functioned.[13] Another alternative is to analyse hierarchies, conflicts, and aspects of power. The analyses will then focus on how different forms of knowledge have been evaluated relative to each other, and which people have had the authority to decide what knowledge is in various historical contexts. Thereby it can be demonstrated how something is elevated to being knowledge – or demoted to being ignorance.[14]

Our own basic position is that knowledge is a socially anchored form of knowing. Such knowledge can be more or less changeable, dispersed, and used in different places and at different times. But by focusing on the roles, meanings, prerequisites, and consequences of knowledge, a better understanding of past societies is made possible. For us this exploration is a key driving force. What we want to know more about is how human societies have functioned in the past. The history of knowledge provides us with a fruitful approach to this issue.[15]

1.2 The History of Knowledge – An Integrative Field

In recent decades, historical scholarship has expanded significantly. Far more people are doing historical research today than in the twentieth century. Furthermore, the subject has broadened thematically, geographically, and chronologically. National research communities remain important, but international fora and venues are even more essential for many historical researchers. In addition, the field of history has, like other disciplines, seen increasing specialisation. Many of today's more innovative studies and dynamic research discussions occur in sub-disciplines or interdisciplinary fields. However, this does not always happen in dialogue with the subject of history itself, and often pioneering and important research has not had a significant impact on broader forms of historical writing. For example, undergraduate

---

[13] Verburgt and Burke, 'Introduction'.
[14] Daston, 'History'; Proctor and Schiebinger, *Agnotology*. [15] Lässig, 'History'.

students of history are still taught about the scientific revolution, although today's historians of science have agreed for decades that such a phenomenon never actually occurred.[16]

Against this background, we have argued for the idea that the history of knowledge should attempt to fill an integrative function.[17] This would be valuable not only to the broader field of history but also to its many sub-disciplines. Our ambition is for the history of knowledge to build bridges between various fields and act as a venue for researchers who are interested in knowledge as a social and historical phenomenon.

But what research traditions do historians of knowledge gain inspiration from and interact with? First, we wish to foreground the historical paradigm of cultural history, or *The New Cultural History*, as it was called in an influential 1989 anthology edited by American historian Lynn Hunt. Cultural history developed from the social history of the 1960s and 1970s with its interest in the history of broad strata of the population. But unlike social history, cultural history was not quantitatively oriented, and cultural historians were primarily interested in the ideas, practices, experiences, and conceptions shared by many people. In the French *Annales* school, this was spoken of in terms of *mentalities*. By studying court records, saints' lives, the weekly press, and folk tales, attempts were made to analyse cultures of the past. The idea was that under-standing cultural beliefs was necessary in order to explain people's actions and historical development. Culture was not only a 'superstructure' on a material economic base, as Karl Marx and his social historical interpreters claimed. Rather, the reverse was true.[18]

Language was central to the new cultural history. In the discipline of history, one therefore sometimes refers synonymously to the linguistic and cultural turns. Inspired by anthropologists such as Clifford Geertz, attempts were made to 'read' human acts and rituals like texts.[19] Through qualitative analysis, it was pointed out how words and language structured human thinking and made possible – or impossible – various collective actions. What stories cause people to start a revolution? What discourses support treating ethnic or religious minorities differently? What concepts govern politics, and how do these change over time?

This type of question proved very productive. Following Michel Foucault, cultural historians have studied discourses, subject positions, and the disciplin-ary function of knowledge. Others, influenced by conceptual historians such as Reinhart Koselleck, have investigated how key political concepts have become

---

[16] Shapin, *Scientific*; Secord, 'Inventing'.   [17] Östling and Larsson Heidenblad, 'Fulfilling'.
[18] Hunt, *New*.   [19] Geertz, *Interpretation*.

charged with meaning and made actions possible. Historians of early modern culture have shown a great deal of interest in religion and religious worldviews. Historians of the modern age and contemporary history have turned to popular culture and new source material such as film, TV, and radio. Also, collective memories and historical stories that create meaning have attracted much attention.

When the history of knowledge began to expand in the years following the turn of the millennium, cultural history was almost regarded as the mainstream approach. Its leading representatives began to discuss how research could be developed further and renewed. In 1999, the above-mentioned Lynn Hunt and two colleagues edited a new anthology entitled *Beyond the Cultural Turn*.[20] Peter Burke – who had been central to the formation of the new cultural history – began to explore new fields, including the history of media and, later, the history of knowledge. The cultural-historical paradigm was and still is very significant. The history of knowledge is an integral part of the same research tradition and also contains visible traces of the social historical impulses that preceded the new cultural history. There is a programmatic interest in studying knowledge as a social phenomenon, and in investigating its importance in and for broader social strata.

Alongside the new cultural history, we will highlight three other sources of inspiration for the history of knowledge. The first is a cluster of fields consisting of the history of science, intellectual history, science and technology studies, and the specifically Nordic disciplinary construct known as the history of ideas (*idé- och lärdomshistoria*).[21] These are dynamic fields that have long had knowledge and the production of knowledge among their primary objects of study. Since the 1970s and 1980s, they have been strongly influenced by sociological and cultural-historical perspectives. Scholars have studied extensively how scientific experiments were conducted, analysed how reputations were established, and followed laboratory personnel in real-time. In parallel, the geographical focus has also broadened to include the entire world, and the chronology has been expanded to include many other forms of knowledge than modern natural science and medicine. The history of science as a concept has been problematised, and is in certain camps considered Eurocentric and teleological.

Against this background, the history of knowledge has been launched as an alternative to the history of science. Influential researchers such as Lorraine Daston have suggested that this is a more accurate term for what contemporary historians of science actually do. From this perspective, the history of

---

[20] Bonnell, *Beyond.*   [21] Jansson, 'Things'.

knowledge is a new name for an already existing research practice. If so, it is not substantially new. This has been a common objection to the history of knowledge from our Nordic colleagues in the history of ideas. 'What is actually new?' has been their question.[22]

We have asserted that the history of knowledge represents an expansion and a shift in emphasis. Among other things, we have highlighted an ambition to write more comprehensive histories of society. We have also pointed out that the history of knowledge encompasses additional forms of knowledge – for example, financial, religious, and practical everyday knowledge. We have argued programmatically that a shift in perspective occurs when we move the focus from the production to the circulation of knowledge in society. During the 2020s, several studies have been published that attempt to demonstrate what this means in practice.[23]

The other group of research specialisations that have influenced the history of knowledge are the histories of media, books, and information. These fields characteristically have a deep interest in media, its functions and materiality. Media can refer to traditional mass media, such as the press, radio, and TV, but also to anything that has a mediating function: maps, terrestrial globes, matchboxes, and statistical investigations. Special interest has been paid to the invention and breakthroughs of new media. During such periods, there are often open negotiations about what the medium is and what it does. Over time, media tend to become normalised and culturally invisible. What is important at a particular time is thus not necessarily that which provokes great discussion. TV and newspapers did not disappear because the Internet and social media disrupted the playing field.[24]

The history of books focuses on a specific medium rather than an entire media system. However, the book as a medium has always been – and still is today – entirely central to the production and circulation of knowledge. The point of departure for historians of books is that books are not empty containers of text. Analysing their appearance, design, and pricing is important for understanding their wider significance. Put differently, it is not enough to read what is printed in them. Consequently, historians of books take an interest in the conditions of production, forms of distribution, edition statistics, and market conditions. When the book becomes the centre of attention, much else becomes visible. This is an approach knowledge historians have found fruitful.[25]

---

[22] Daston, 'History'; Bergwik and Holmberg, 'Standing'.

[23] Östling and Larsson Heidenblad, 'Fulfilling'; Larsson Heidenblad, *Environmental*; Östling et al., *Humanister*.

[24] Jülich, *Mediernas*.   [25] Secord, *Visions*.

The third specialisation we wish to highlight as a source of inspiration is the history of education. This field has grown rapidly in recent decades, not least in connection with the education of teachers.[26] Today's historians of education are interested in the school system and higher education, their configuration and governance, but also in the training that occurs in other fields, for instance through campaigns or in non-profit organisations and companies. A good deal of research within the history of education typically foregrounds learning processes and their prerequisites. The emphasis here is on the education of children and young people. In contradistinction, the other specialisations we have highlighted tend to have adults as a central focus, albeit rarely older adults. The history of knowledge finds the education of young people interesting for several reasons, one being that it presents opportunities for analysing how knowledge circulates over time and among generations.[27]

A minor specialisation that is closely connected to the history of education is the history of professions. Researchers within this field are interested in how professions are established, and how their members – lawyers, doctors, nurses, social workers, etc. – are trained and collectively maintain their positions in society. These professional groups are in close contact with specific scientific fields and institutions of higher education. Through their professional activities, they are bearers of knowledge which they put into circulation in society. Like the history of education, the history of professions also provides opportunities for the analysis of circulation over time.[28]

Taken together, the cultural history paradigm and the three major specialisations we have highlighted provide both a foundation and a set of interfaces for the history of knowledge. So far, it has primarily been with and among these fields that discussions have been held, exchanges made, and new research questions formulated. The function filled by the history of knowledge varies. In relation to cultural history, it is a narrowing and a focusing of the object of study – but in relation to other fields it is rather a way to pose broader questions: What is its significance beyond the academy? How does it relate to the major social changes of the time? What happens if we combine x with the contemporary phenomena of y and z?

From a broader scholarly perspective, it is not wrong to claim that the history of knowledge has so far mainly fulfilled an *intradisciplinary* rather than an *interdisciplinary* function. In other words, historians of knowledge have above all bridged gaps between various sub-disciplines of historical scholarship and, to a lesser degree, established new collaborations with other scholars in the

---

[26] Westberg, 'Bright'.   [27] Barnes and Pietsch, 'History'; Lundberg, 'Exploring'.
[28] Slagstad and Messel, *Profesjonshistorier.*

humanities and social sciences who deal with 'knowledge studies' in, for instance, anthropology, philosophy, sociology, psychology, law, political science, and comparative literature. We feel that in future it would be desirable to have more genuinely interdisciplinary exchanges, and that there is a great unexploited potential here.

1.3 The Main Specialisations of the History of Knowledge

The recent strong development of the history of knowledge nevertheless risks overshadowing the fact that there are several competing ideas about what the field is or should be. After all, the history of knowledge appears today in a number of different guises. When we examine the current landscape of the field, we can distinguish at least five main, sometimes overlapping, specialisations.[29]

First, there is an encyclopaedic variant of the history of knowledge. It is characterised by an all-encompassing ambition rather than by new perspectives or theoretical reasoning. The best examples of this are Peter Burke's general books on the history of knowledge. In *A Social History of Knowledge* (two volumes, 2000 and 2012) he demonstrates being widely read in the history of ideas, culture, and science of the last five hundred years, from Gutenberg to Wikipedia.[30]

In the first chapter of his introductory book *What Is the History of Knowledge?* (2016), Burke presents basic concepts, processes, and problems of the history of knowledge. Building on the two earlier volumes, he also formulates some general reflections on the subject. His starting point is that knowledge exists in various forms in any given culture: pure and applied, explicit and implicit, learned and popular, male and female, local and universal. Against this background, Burke argues that there 'are only histories, in the plural, of knowledges, also in the plural'.[31]

Historians of science suggest a different understanding of the history of knowledge. As previously mentioned, to them it offers a reformulation of the traditional objects of study in their field, thereby challenging established concepts and patterns of interpretation. For example, in several articles Lorraine Daston has described the transformation of the history of science in recent decades. As a result of global and practical developments in the discipline, its methodological repertoire has broadened considerably, and its objects of study have become more diverse. Consequently, many historians of science have distanced themselves from an older, teleological foundational narrative about

---

[29] Östling, 'Circulation, Arenas'.   [30] Burke, *Gutenberg*; Burke, *Encyclopédie*.
[31] Burke, *What Is*, 7.

the evolution of Western science to the degree that a more adequate designation for today's specialisation would, according to Daston, be the history of knowledge. One advantage of this designation is that it is not linked to a particular modern understanding of science, but is capable of encompassing the study of Hellenistic alchemy, pre-Columbian botany in South America, and social science of the post-war era. At the same time, Daston points out, the nebulous character of the history of knowledge is problematic: what does *not* fit into the field?[32]

The field's vagueness has not prevented historians of science from associating themselves with it in recent studies. For instance, Elaine Leong has adopted the history of knowledge as a framework for analysing medicine and science in early modern English households, while Jürgen Renn has used it as a general point of departure in his book *The Evolution of Knowledge* (2020).[33] Another group of historians of science have been inspired by the history of knowledge in applying new perspectives to the history of the Royal Swedish Academy of Sciences.[34]

In a third interpretation, the history of knowledge becomes a field that encompasses the study of all academic forms of knowledge, not only those that have traditionally been a central focus for historians of science, technology, or medicine. The best example here is the renewed interest in the history of the humanities. A key figure is Rens Bod, who has spearheaded writing a more integrative history that extends beyond the study of single humanistic disciplines. In the first issue of the journal *History of Humanities* (2016), he and his colleagues encouraged researchers in the history of the humanities to take an active interest in the history of the natural sciences, and vice versa. 'Eventually', they wrote, 'a case could be made for uniting the history of the humanities and the history of science under the head of "history of knowledge"'.[35]

There are certain recurring themes and approaches in this recent research on the history of the humanities. One type of investigation focuses on studying the formation of the humanities as a distinct field, along with how its relations to other areas of knowledge, particularly the natural sciences, have shifted over time.[36] Another approach applies perspectives from the modern history of science to analyse humanists of the past; one example is using the concept of the persona to investigate ideals and norms prevalent among historians of a particular era.[37] Yet another type of analysis concentrates on the materiality and infrastructure of the humanities, for example archives, libraries, and

---

[32] Daston, 'History'.   [33] Leong, *Recipes*; Renn, *Evolution*.   [34] Kärnfelt, *Knowledge*.
[35] Bod, 'New', 6.   [36] Krämer, 'Shifting'; Hammar and Östh Gustafsson, 'Unity'.
[37] Paul, *How to*.

museums.[38] And finally, researchers, not least Rens Bod himself, assume global perspectives and compare Western to other forms of knowledge.[39]

In a fourth version of the history of knowledge, rational, systematic, or academic knowledge is simply one among several forms of knowledge. Proponents of this specialisation feel that attention should also be paid to tacit and practical knowledge, as well as to indigenous knowledge. Anna Nilsson Hammar has taken, for example, Aristotle's division of knowledge as her point of departure. She emphasises that researchers have hitherto focused on the production and circulation of scientific or rational knowledge (*theoria*), but have devoted less attention to other forms of knowledge (*praxis* and *poiesis*) or to the relationships among these.[40]

A greater multiplicity of forms of knowledge has also been suggested in two journals impacted by the history of knowledge. In the introduction to the first number of *KNOW*, Shadi Bartsch-Zimmer and her co-editors explain that the aim of the journal is 'uncovering and explicating diverse forms of knowledge from antiquity to the present, and accounting for contemporary forms of knowledge in terms of their history, politics, and culture'.[41] In a similar manner, the editors of the *Journal for the History of Knowledge* stated in its initial issue that the journal will be devoted to 'the history of knowledge in its broadest sense', including 'the study of science, but also of indigenous, artisanal and other types of knowledge'. This journal is also meant to offer a platform for contributions that compare Western and non-Western forms of knowledge, or that analyse relationships among concepts and practices from various parts of the world.[42]

Finally, in a fifth understanding of the history of knowledge the emphasis is on knowledge as a basic category in society. One common denominator among those who underline the role and relevance of knowledge in society is that they have academic backgrounds in the subject of history, with its traditional focus on politics, social relations, and cultural phenomena. In an early programmatic article from the German-language history of knowledge, 'Was ist Wissensgeschichte?' (2011), Philipp Sarasin emphasises that historians have always wanted to relate to broader contexts and have searched for totalities, be they the nation or society. Consequently, he argues that the history of knowledge should deal with 'the social production and circulation of knowledge', because knowledge moves among different people, groups, and contexts, and can in principle cross institutional, social, political, and geographical boundaries. This is not the same thing as the free dissemination and the even distribution of

---

[38] Pyle, 'Forum'.   [39] Bod, *World*.   [40] Nilsson Hammar, 'Theoria'.
[41] Bartsch, 'Introduction'.   [42] 'About', *JHoK*.

knowledge, but it means that knowledge by its very nature can be transmitted, put into circulation, and interact in other fields of knowledge in various social contexts.[43]

In another programmatic article, Simone Lässig discusses what the history of knowledge has to offer historical research in general. She considers the field a version of social and cultural history that investigates knowledge as a phenomenon that impacts nearly every aspect of human life. Her view of knowledge and society is clear in her concluding sentences: 'The history of knowledge does not emphasize knowledge instead of society but rather seeks to analyse and comprehend knowledge *in* society and knowledge *in* culture. Approaching society and culture in all their complexity, the history of knowledge will broaden and deepen our understanding of how humans have created knowledge over the course of the past.'[44]

The five understandings of the history of knowledge described here are quite general: there are no discrete lines of demarcation among them, and none represents a well-defined research programme. If anything, they illustrate the fact that the history of knowledge is capable of attracting followers from many different academic disciplines, and that the specific knowledge-historical form adopted is determined by the intellectual and scholarly tradition the researcher in question belongs to and wants to promote.

Nevertheless, the differences matter to the histories we write and explore. Returning to the digital revolution, Silicon Valley, and Andrew Grove, with which this section began, researchers can approach these phenomena in many different ways. Those who are interested in worlds of learning and scientific progress will study Stanford University and the Massachusetts Institute of Technology, as well as the pioneers of computer science, such as Claude Shannon or Alan Turing. Those who wish to write more comprehensive histories of society will use different chronologies and give other people centre stage. Perhaps, they will foreground Steve Jobs, Bill Gates, and the introduction of personal computers into the home in the 1980s and 1990s. Perhaps they will begin even later, in 1997, when *Time Magazine* named Andrew Grove the 'Man of the Year'. The perspective will shift even more for those who are mainly interested in politics or society's infrastructure. These historians may want to study the spread of computers in schools or the expansion of broadband networks. What interests encouraged these developments, and why? Were they connected to visions of a future information and knowledge society? Yet, other researchers may analyse the evolution and dissemination of programming

---

[43] Sarasin, 'Was ist', 165.   [44] Lässig, 'History', 58.

languages, business concepts such as 'the lean start-up', or how different generations of young people have learned to play video games.

What is obviously interesting and stimulating to one historian of knowledge is not necessarily so to another. But what unites researchers in the field is a desire to historicise, explore, and analyse what knowledge has been and has meant in the past. The question is what analytic tools and concepts we can use. Let us explore some of them.

2 Key Concepts in the History of Knowledge: Circulation, Actor, and Institution

In this section, we introduce three key concepts in the history of knowledge: *circulation*, *actor*, and *institution*. We explain their meanings and anchor them in their respective historiographical traditions. Above all, we attempt to show how they can be productive for the study of the history of knowledge, and to demonstrate their analytical potential.

2.1 The Circulation of Knowledge

Historians of the twenty-first century, like other cultural and social researchers, have ended up ever more often studying interactions, interweavings, and patterns of movement. This increased interest can reasonably be linked to the globalisation of the last few decades, but the digital revolution also gives these subjects a high degree of topicality. In recent years, a good deal of attention has been paid to how knowledge is formed and reformed when it is in motion. Historians who tackle these questions have different interests and come from varying historiographical traditions. Nevertheless, it is possible to discern a convergence towards certain common problems, and an increasing number of scholars have begun to embrace a common concept: *circulation*.[45]

Circulation has become one of the most popular concepts in the history of knowledge. Joel Barnes has aptly spoken of it 'as something of a master-concept', at least in certain parts of the field.[46] Historians have used it frequently in order to provide a more complex understanding of the processes of knowledge, not least in order to break down overly simple dichotomies such as centre–periphery, sender–receiver, and producer–user. The premise here is that circulating knowledge is in a state of potential change. This means that words like *diffusion*, *dissemination*, and *mediation* are problematic because they imply that what is in motion is actually fixed.[47]

---

[45] Östling et al., *Circulation.*   [46] Barnes, 'Knowledge'.
[47] Raj, 'Beyond'; Östling et al., *Circulation.*

In circulation studies, knowledge is instead considered dynamic. More concretely, analyses often focus on what happens when knowledge moves among different places, genres, and formats, but also on investigating the main material and media preconditions that exist at a given time. Furthermore, the concept of circulation contributes to a basic shift of perspective in the study of knowledge, from production to circulation. It is no longer the creation of and the conditions for new knowledge that are being observed, but how knowledge is used, how it moves, and how it is transformed. In addition, a circulation perspective entails a broadening of the view of the knowledge process so that other types of actors and historical contexts can be introduced into the analysis.[48]

Many of the foundational discussions on the circulation of knowledge have taken place in the history of science (and in part also, if from different points of departure, in the discipline of communication studies). An important impetus came from James A. Secord's article 'Knowledge in Transit' (2004). This text can be characterised as a polemical programme statement for a new kind of history of science, one which does not put the study of the production of scientific knowledge at the forefront. Instead, Secord encouraged his colleagues to direct their analytic interest towards questions about knowledge in motion: What happens when knowledge circulates? How is it transformed from a concern for particular individuals to something that larger groups of people take for granted?[49]

According to Secord the most important development in the history of science in recent decades is that science has begun to be studied as a practical and situated activity. The predominant approach has been investigating in detail how particular actors have produced knowledge. The concreteness of the many case studies has contributed to the demystification of scientific activities, but the wider social significance of what is being analysed often remains unclear. Therefore, Secord encouraged historians of science to place as much weight on analysing audiences, readers, and media as they have on investigating voyages of discovery, laboratories, and experiments.[50] According to Secord, all scientific activity should be considered a form of communication. He further stressed that historians of science have been far too 'obsessed with novelty', and have therefore been inclined to analyse origins, producers, and innovations. What happens to knowledge later has often been considered less important, and there has thus been a tendency to describe it cursorily after the main analysis has been completed.[51]

'Knowledge in Transit' has made a significant impression in the two decades since its publication. It is frequently cited and often used in introductory

---

[48] Ibid.   [49] Secord, 'Knowledge'.   [50] Ibid.   [51] Ibid.

discussions on choosing objects of study and approaches. And although one cannot discern a radical turn away from the study of the production of knowledge, there is no doubt that today many researchers with different specialisations are interested in how knowledge circulates.

Historians of the early modern global history of science are one example. To them, the circulation concept has become a tool for challenging a powerful Eurocentric narrative of 'the scientific revolution'. According to this narrative, the modern natural sciences were born in Europe, only to thereafter spread to the rest of the world through colonial expansion. This story is intimately connected to classical modernisation theory and a unidirectional model of diffusion, where scientific knowledge is spread from the centre to the periphery because it is rational, true, and practically useful. Applying a circulation perspective allows this type of interpretation to be questioned. Researchers who have studied the history of European empires have, for instance, shown how important indigenous actors in the colonies were for processes of knowledge. There was never a scientific paradigm spreading frictionlessly from Cambridge, Leiden, or Montpellier to Bombay, Batavia, or Saigon. Knowledge was transformed when encountering local traditions of thought, social orders, and power hierarchies.[52]

Consequently, the circulation concept can be used in order to show how knowledge moves geographically, socially, chronologically, and through media and networks. Its analytical power lies in providing a concrete alternative to simple dissemination models, which many researchers view with scepticism. The concept of circulation thus complicates questions on how knowledge is produced and how it becomes significant. The most radical voices actually question the principle of dissemination itself and the idea that knowledge has a point of origin. According to this view, production and circulation are inseparable.[53]

Despite the analytical merits of the concept of circulation, there remains a problem: the concept is and remains elastic. Kapil Raj has characterised it as a 'recurrent, though non-theorized, concept', while James A. Secord – who himself directed attention to knowledge in motion – has recently claimed that the term risks being reduced to a 'meaningless buzzword'.[54] In a similar way, Philipp Sarasin and Andreas Kilcher have pointed out that circulation has become a catchword that can include almost any type of movement.[55]

We share this criticism of the concept of circulation, but feel that it should not be discarded altogether. On the contrary, we propose proceeding from more

---

[52] Lightman, McOuat, and Stewart, *Circulation*; Findlen, *Empires*; Secord, 'Inventing'.
[53] Sarasin, 'Was ist'.   [54] Raj, *Relocating*, 225; Secord, 'Knowledge'; Secord, 'Project'.
[55] Sarasin and Kilcher, 'Editorial', 7–11.

limited and explicitly defined understandings of movements of knowledge. One of these we call the *societal circulation of knowledge*. The starting point here is that knowledge is studied as a broader societal phenomenon. In order for something to become the object of circulation analyses of this kind, it must have a certain societal relevance and reach. That which concerns only a few individuals or small groups of people is not central. This means, among other things, that scientific discoveries are of secondary importance while the focus is on substantial breakthroughs of knowledge that have an effect in wider social, economic, political, and cultural contexts.[56] Like historians such as Philipp Sarasin and Simone Lässig, we build here on an older societal historical programme, and argue that the study of knowledge in society provides important entry points to history.[57]

In various studies, we have investigated how knowledge has circulated in society. Among other things, we have analysed how environmental issues went from being a concern for a small group of experts and scientists to becoming a public concern around 1970, but we have also charted the more general preconditions for the circulation of knowledge in the public sphere of the postwar era (in Section 3, we provide more detailed examples of how we have studied this kind of societal circulation of knowledge).

The movement of knowledge in past societies can, however, be investigated in many other ways. Erik Bodensten has, for instance, tackled the question of when knowledge about potatoes became more widespread in eighteenth-century Sweden. He shows that this was not a linear, cumulative process of diffusion, but that a distinct breakthrough of knowledge took place around 1749–1750, largely because a special network, which had long eagerly promoted potatoes, now gained control over important institutions and means of communication. Because of this, broader groups in society became aware of the relevance of potatoes, and a collective knowledge process was set in motion.[58] Måns Ahlstedt Åberg investigates how knowledge circulated between the Swedish State Institute for Racial Biology and the Swedish general public in the 1930s. He demonstrates that there were exchanges of knowledge in both directions between the Institute and ordinary Swedes who participated in a major genealogical project.[59]

Historians can investigate the preconditions for the societal circulation of knowledge in various ways. For example, scholars have attempted to map the systems and platforms that provide historically specific prerequisites that set knowledge in motion. One analytical concept in this context is the *knowledge*

---

[56] Östling and Larsson Heidenblad, 'Fulfilling'.   [57] Sarasin, 'Was ist'; Lässig, 'History'.
[58] Bodensten, 'Societal'.   [59] Ahlstedt Åberg, 'Amateur'.

arena. This can be understood as a place that, within its particular framework, offers an opportunity and sets boundaries for the circulation of knowledge. It functions as a meeting place or venue for a certain kind of knowledge actor and a certain type of audience. In order for an arena to promote the societal circulation of knowledge, it normally must have a measure of stability and permanence, even if the content of the knowledge that circulates in a particular arena can vary over time.[60]

The boundary between a knowledge arena and a knowledge institution can be difficult to maintain. In many cases, however, the degree of formalisation or regulation differs, because a knowledge institution tends to be a part of the established educational system or the scientific community. The status of an arena is also wholly dependent on how it is perceived by its contemporaries. There is thus a subjective aspect: a knowledge arena comes into existence and endures because certain groups perceive it as a place for the exchange and transmission of certain types of knowledge. Periodicals, TV programmes, book series, and social media accounts can fulfil such functions – but do not necessarily do so. What makes the concept especially useful is that it enables comparisons across space and time, which may make visible the shifting preconditions for the social circulation of knowledge.

Seen from this broader perspective, the knowledge arena is connected to the concept of *infrastructure.* By this is meant the basic preconditions for a society's communication and mediation of knowledge, for instance the existence of a press corps, the art of printing, a school system, and postal services. This can also include the social structure of a society, and the opportunities various groups have for taking part in the main processes of knowledge. In times past, much of this infrastructure was oral, informal, and local, which means that historians of knowledge face certain difficulties. Nevertheless, recent research shows that also less well-off strata are rewarding objects of study on the basis of perspectives drawn from the history of knowledge. Because of material limitations, creative research approaches emerge that expand our understanding of people of the past.[61]

Overall, the circulation concept is one of the most productive in the history of knowledge. It has proven useful for many different types of studies in various contexts, geographical spaces, and historical epochs. Accordingly, there is also an obvious risk that it becomes a watered-down concept, but, as we have emphasised, the way forward is not to abandon it but to specify the kind of knowledge in motion being foregrounded and how it can be investigated. More

---

[60] Östling, 'Circulation'.   [61] Nilsson Hammar and Norrhem, 'Capacity'.

generally, circulation offers a perspective on how the history of knowledge can be studied, and how knowledge processes can open up to multifaceted analyses.

2.2 Knowledge Actors

Every land and every era has its allotted share of biographies of prominent scientists, intellectuals, and educational reformers. Nevertheless, it is not misleading to claim that the theoretical currents that have influenced historical and sociological studies of knowledge since the 1960s have emphasised structures rather than actors, collectives rather than individuals. This is true for Karl Mannheim's and Ludwik Fleck's concept of a *Denkstil*, Thomas S. Kuhn's concept of a *paradigm*, and Michel Foucault's concept of an *épistémè*, and also for the concepts of later theoreticians such as Pierre Bourdieu, Donna Haraway, and Bruno Latour.[62]

Despite all the innovative research that these influential thinkers have given rise to, there is a risk that the history of knowledge becomes anonymous unless individuals are allowed to be the subjects of narratives. Suzanne Marchand has expressed this fear and criticised a tradition in the histories of knowledge and science that she calls 'Foucauldian structuralism' with 'its erasure of individual biographies and intentions'. Marchand asks, 'is there room in the history of knowledge for an approach that privileges not the knowledge making as such but the wider context and the peculiarities of the knowers?'[63] We would like to think so. To us, knowledge is always socially anchored, and in order to understand its dynamics different kinds of knowledge actors must be afforded space in the analyses.

A knowledge actor can be described as a person who, in a particular historical context, contributes to producing and/or circulating knowledge. Under certain circumstances, various kinds of audiences can also be included in the *actor* concept; they then become co-creators in the knowledge process. Knowledge actors can be studied using social history as a point of departure, for example by analysing their societal positions and various forms of capital. This type of study is relatively common, but, as Philipp Sarasin points out, an investigation that stops here risks demonstrating a kind of sociological reductionism. He asserts that the study of knowledge actors should also include the content and form of the knowledge in question. Thus, an individual's capacity and authority to act as a knowledge actor also depends on the theoretical and practical knowledge that the individual possesses or transmits.[64]

---

[62] Östling, Larsson Heidenblad, and Nilsson Hammar, *Knowledge Actors*.
[63] Marchand, 'Weighing', 144–5.   [64] Sarasin, 'Was ist'".

In our own investigations into the history of knowledge, we have emphasised the significance of knowledge actors. David Larsson Heidenblad has, in a study of the breakthrough of environmental issues in post-war Sweden, argued that around 1970 several historical actors were putting new issues on the agenda and setting new knowledge in motion. 'In my view, the social breakthrough of knowledge occurred because specific people did specific things at specific times, which triggered chain reactions', writes Larsson Heidenblad. In his study, the central knowledge actors are chemist Hans Palmstierna, journalist Barbro Soller, and historian Birgitta Odén, but he also broadens the scope to include environmental activists, upper secondary school teachers, and students. Overall, he exposes broad societal processes of knowledge and the roles played by various actors.[65]

In a similar way, Johan Östling, Anton Jansson, and Ragni Svensson Stringberg have foregrounded knowledge actors in studying the circulation of humanistic knowledge in post-war society. In their account, columnists, researchers, authors, and intellectuals are significant, but so too are managers of publishing companies, TV entrepreneurs, periodical editors, organisers of public education, and sundry other persons. These humanist knowledge actors had varying backgrounds, profiles, and functions, but were active, individually or together, in public knowledge arenas. Often these actors had university educations in the humanities, and not a few had completed a doctorate, but people who lacked academic experience were also important for the humanities in the public sphere during the post-war decades.[66]

One important message in our studies is that co-operation among a number of different actors is required for knowledge to be set in motion. Who these actors are varies from one era to another. This means that historians of knowledge must investigate particular role distributions and constellations. Individuals are thus significant as knowledge actors, but they are never alone. Of this, we are convinced.

Our approach is consistent with the main points of departure for the circulation of knowledge described earlier. For example, Lissa Roberts maintains that circulation should not be understood as having to do with something being moved from a central to a local context only to later return to its point of origin. She feels instead that circulation should be used to avoid privileged positions that are taken for granted, such as European metropoles and learned societies.[67] Similarly, Kapil Raj affirms that the strength of a circulation perspective is that it gives an actor's role to all those involved in knowledge processes. By this, he

---

[65] Larsson Heidenblad, *Environmental Turn*, 20–1.
[66] Östling, Jansson, and Svensson Stringberg, *Humanister*.   [67] Roberts, 'Situating', 18.

does not mean that the power and opportunities of historical actors are evenly distributed – on the contrary – but he does maintain that a circulation analysis is an advantageous way to empirically investigate these power relationships, rather than assuming that there exists a certain relationship of dominance that consistently manifests itself in particular ways.[68]

Raj and his colleagues have developed a vocabulary for analysing a broader repertoire of actors. Using concepts like *go-betweens*, *intermediaries*, and *brokers of knowledge*, they have been able to capture the dynamics and hier-archies of various knowledge processes.[69] They have often taken colonial connections as a starting point, wishing to problematise the relationship between presumed centres and peripheries, although the concepts can also be used in other contexts, for example to demonstrate the multiplicity of actors involved in the production and circulation of knowledge.

This type of concept can also be used to study other phenomena. For instance, historian of education Johannes Westberg has discussed nineteenth-century teachers using the concept of *knowledge brokers* as a point of departure (a concept he has taken from researchers in the educational and health sciences). It is obvious that teachers worked in classrooms and taught children, but Westberg is interested in their other roles as knowledge actors. Many of them, not least in the countryside, had other mandates as well, for example in political bodies, libraries, or banks. As knowledge brokers they could be confident in the authority they had as teachers, while they simultaneously functioned as bridge builders between the educational system and other sectors of society. Using this analytical concept, a multifaceted picture emerges of teachers from that time.[70]

Another way of approaching knowledge actors is through network or field analyses of various kinds. One tradition, inspired by Pierre Bourdieu among others, reveals how individuals are included in various groups based on the social or cultural capital they possess. These networks are vital for maintaining systems of power and promoting careers. Elite schools and top universities have become the objects for many studies of this kind.[71] Other researchers use digital tools to map the relationships and patterns of movement of knowledge actors. In one large project, the early modern European Republic of Letters was visualised using the voluminous correspondences of, among others, famous and lesser-known philosophers and scholars.[72] Another method of analysing networks is that employed by Harald Fischer-Tiné. One of his books investigates medical history in Colonial India, specifically the parallel formation of Western colonial medicine and the transformation of local South Asian varieties of the healing

[68] Raj, 'Beyond'.   [69] Raj, 'Go-Betweens'; Findlen, *Empires*.
[70] Westberg, 'Knowledge Brokers'.   [71] Bourdieu, *Homo academicus*.
[72] Edelstein et al., 'Historical Research'.

arts in the nineteenth century. He concludes that medical knowledge developed in *polycentric communication networks*, a concept he deploys to pluralise a centre–periphery model that otherwise risks giving the impression that all significant knowledge production occurred in a metropole (London, Edinburgh, Oxford) while the colonies supplied only the raw materials of science. He argues instead that Bombay and Calcutta were what Bruno Latour has called *centres of calculation* – central locations for knowledge generation with their own authoritative networks. Because standards regulating South Asian scientific practice were different from and less strict than those in Great Britain, new and sometimes unconventional methods were given greater latitude, thereby benefiting the development of medical knowledge.[73]

Knowledge-historical studies of actors can, however, just as well focus on other domains than science or medicine. Anna Nilsson Hammar and Svante Norrhem have investigated servants in noble households in the seventeenth century. By analysing supplications from servants to their masters, these two historians demonstrate that a significant amount of both theoretical and practical knowledge – such as administrative, legal, and economic knowledge – was required to navigate these households and thereby maintain or improve one's position.[74] Researchers in the history of childhood and youth have explored the roles younger persons may have played as knowledge actors. For instance, Björn Lundberg argues that students were important actors in creating awareness of global issues in the 1960s. He demonstrates how school campaigns contributed to setting knowledge in motion.[75]

The perspective of power is central in many investigations of history's knowledge actors. For example, there has long been a feminist current in the history of science. Susan Leigh Star and Margaret W. Rossiter are among those who took an early interest in gendered structures in the academy. Since then several gender historical studies have demonstrated how the traditional male professor was dependent on other knowledge actors for his work, not infrequently more or less invisible women. Typical examples from the natural sciences include a celebrated male professor's human computers and laboratory assistants, who were never mentioned at the publication of an epoch-making scientific work.[76] A particular variant of this social order was 'the scientific family'. Within the framework of marriage, a couple could engage in a kind of scientific teamwork, but there was no doubt about who ranked highest and enjoyed the most prestige, even when the wife also possessed solid academic qualifications. Additionally, it was long expected that a professor's wife would

---

[73] Fischer-Tiné, *Pidgin-Knowledge*.   [74] Nilsson Hammar and Norrhem, 'Capacity'.
[75] Lundberg, 'Youth Activism'.   [76] Star, 'Sociology'; Rossiter, *Women*.

not only be her husband's assistant or secretary, but that she would also assume the role of hostess at dinners and other representational functions in the home.[77]

An important concept in many newer studies of knowledge actors is the *scientific persona*. This concept, as defined by Lorraine Daston and H. Otto Sibum, can be seen as a kind of cultural identity that materialises at the intersection of an individual's biography and a societal institution. The persona influences the individual's body and mind while simultaneously forming a collective; it designates a species rather than a person. A scientific persona – whether an instrument maker, a technocrat, or an independent scholar – takes shape in a specific historical context, but may undergo changes. At any given moment, the number of possible forms is, however, clearly limited.[78] Herman Paul has approached personae in the humanities in a similar manner, singling out what holds a scholarly persona together, such as common virtues, skills, and desires.[79] In a study of Marie Curie, Eva Hemmungs Wirtén has also used the persona concept to analyse the construction of the world's best-known female researcher. Additionally, her book is a good example of how historians, when focusing on one person, can get at so much more than a single individual, in this case everything from intellectual property to celebrity culture.[80] And of course the persona concept can also be applied to other types of knowledge actors, not just scientists.

Most knowledge-historical studies of actors seem to be synchronic – that is, they investigate how individuals or collectives functioned as knowledge actors in one particular era. However, it is quite possible to also imagine diachronic studies that follow change and continuity for a certain type of actor over longer periods of time. In this spirit, Peter Burke has written a book on the polymath as a historical type, from Leonardo da Vinci to Susan Sontag. He identifies five hundred people who can be classified as polymaths, but he is not content with creating a group portrait of some of the most colourful individuals from the history of learning. Instead, Burke examines details and uncovers larger patterns in the history of advanced knowledge. On the basis of the polymath as a knowledge actor, he illuminates the shifting conditions of the formation of knowledge from the fifteenth to the twenty-first centuries, not least comprehensive questions concerning the necessity and curse of specialisation.[81]

In several studies, Sven Dupré and his colleagues have also adopted longer temporal perspectives to study the skills and capacities of various knowledge actors. In an anthology he co-edited with Christine Göttler, attention is focused on the intricate relationship between knowledge and discernment in early

---

[77] Berg, Florin, and Wisselgren, *Par i vetenskap.*   [78] Daston and Sibum, 'Introduction'.
[79] Paul, *How to Be.*   [80] Hemmungs Wirtén, *Making.*   [81] Burke, *Polymath.*

modern artists' communities and learned circles. Discernment was linked to a special ability to discover the secrets of nature or existence, and was considered a kind of knowledge restricted to genuine experts in various artistic and scientific fields.[82]

In other words, there are multiple analytic possibilities for studying knowledge actors. We therefore doubt the validity of Suzanne Marchand's fears about the persistence of a primacy of structures in the history of knowledge. Nevertheless, the history of knowledge must also study other objects than individuals and their lives. It is therefore high time we move on to a discussion of the institutions of knowledge.

2.3 The Institutions of Knowledge

Institutions have long been an object of study for those of us interested in the history of knowledge. In the history of education preschools, schools, and folk high schools (independent adult education colleges) have received much attention; historians of science have concentrated on academies, research institutes, and laboratories; historians of books and media have written about archives, libraries, and museums; and political scientists and historians of politics have examined committee reports and parliamentary processes. These institutions of knowledge are often part of an established educational system, a scientific community, or political or cultural life. Elementary schools, teacher training colleges for women, and the university were, for instance, institutions of knowledge at certain times in modern history within a shared institutional system, where they constituted interdependent and interacting parts of a relatively well-delimited unit.[83]

However, a knowledge-historical perspective can also here contribute to increased understanding of a phenomenon, enabling us to see new connections. Not all institutions of knowledge have been components of formalised educational or scientific systems. The monastic system, established in the fifth and sixth centuries in France and Italy, originated in the eastern parts of the Roman Empire and in the Middle East. Older historiography often emphasised the spiritual and social functions of the monasteries, but based on the premises of this book they can equally well be considered knowledge institutions. Many monasteries acquired significant book collections, and because of their libraries, a good deal of learning survived the tumultuous events of late antiquity and the early Middle Ages. Furthermore, monasteries' scriptoria were vital for securing the production of books; in many regions, especially from the ninth to the

---

[82] Dupré and Göttler, *Knowledge.*   [83] Glückler, Suddaby, and Lenz, *Knowledge.*

beginning of the thirteenth centuries, they had in practice a monopoly on the production of books.[84]

As always, a historian of knowledge can also focus on other epochs and phenomena. In the later part of the nineteenth century, think tanks began to appear in the United Kingdom, mainly with a focus on economic issues. These gradually became meeting places for politicians, researchers, and opinion leaders. After World War II, several American think tanks were established, many functioning as tools in the ideological and intellectual struggle of the Cold War. Since the 1980s, the number of thinks tanks has increased in many parts of the world. According to reports, there are today over 11,000 brain trusts with various political, scientific, and religious overtones. Some of these produce knowledge in a strict sense, while others concentrate on circulating particular types of information and forming opinions. But are these think tanks truly institutions of knowledge? Should we not rather see them as knowledge arenas of the kind introduced in the previous section, that is, as places that within a given framework offer opportunities for and set limits on the circulation of knowledge? And is it mainly knowledge that think tanks are interested in – are they not equally often promoting an ideological line, developing policy, or even spreading propaganda? A knowledge historian can profitably pose such questions.

A knowledge-historical approach can on a more fundamental level contribute to revising previously accepted interpretations of the development of well-established knowledge institutions. A classic institution to study is the university. In historiography, the university appears as an entirely European institution, whose beginnings can be traced back to Bologna and Paris in the High Middle Ages. An example of this is the introduction to *A History of the University in Europe*, where it is claimed that mediaeval European universities were 'indisputably an original institution' that 'gradually spread to the whole of Europe and then to the whole world'.[85]

Recently an alternative historiography has begun to take shape. Two researchers of education, Roy Lowe and Yoshihito Yasuhara, are pioneers in this field. In their book *The Origins of Higher Learning*, they depict the rise of European universities in the twelfth century as the end point of a long process that began with the very oldest civilisations of Asia and the Middle East. Their point of departure is that all complex societies in history have had institutions of higher learning, and they thereby combine a global with a knowledge-historical perspective to make visible the significance of different knowledge institutions in the past. These institutions have varied in character and status, but the point

---

[84] Larsen and Rubenson, *Monastic.*   [85] Rüegg and Ridder-Symoens, *History.*

Lowe and Yasuhara make is that all cultures with a certain degree of complexity need institutions that can safeguard, transmit, and – albeit to varying degrees – develop higher learning. From this vantage point, the European university is a specific variant of a more general historical phenomenon. At the same time, they do not deny that mediaeval universities were special, and that they, like no other institution of higher learning, developed into a global prototype in the early modern and modern eras.[86]

Inspired by Lowe and Yasuhara, it is thus possible to write history in which the university becomes only one example of an institution of higher learning. In order to understand its emergence and identify what was new in Europe of the High Middle Ages, it is useful to compare it with older institutions of knowledge. Precursors can be found in the Classical Mediterranean world. In Athens of the fifth and fourth centuries BCE, a more cohesive constellation of institutions of knowledge emerged. The first more permanent school was Plato's Academy, where multiple subjects were taught. After his death, Plato's disciples continued his work. At the same time, the Mouseion, one of antiquity's foremost centres of learning, was founded in Alexandria. Here philosophers and other thinkers conducted research financed by the Ptolemies. Overall, these and other knowledge institutions had a very significant impact. Libraries, academies, and other educational establishments here acquired a form that became a model for later eras, not least in mediaeval and Renaissance Europe.[87]

Institutions of higher learning were obviously not only Western innovations. In the middle of the first millennium BCE, several centres of learning were founded on the Indian subcontinent along the two northern rivers, the Ganges and the Indus. These areas were characterised by political, religious, and cultural diversity, but the spread of Buddhism in the fifth and fourth centuries BCE contributed to a more widespread and more unified way of thinking in southern and south-eastern Asia. Several Buddhist monasteries were founded and some became intellectual power centres, for example Taxila in today's Pakistan and Nalanda in present-day India. Further north in China, other institutions of knowledge developed, not least along the Huang He. Especially the latter part of the Zhou dynasty, 770–256 BCE, was characterised by scientific curiosity and intellectual vitality. In the fifth century BCE, Confucius quickly gathered a large group of followers, and because of them his ideas became foundational for Chinese society, despite his never establishing his own institution of learning. There were, however, other physical centres of higher learning. The so-called Jixia Academy, situated in eastern China in present-day Shandong, attracted a large group of learned men of varying philosophical and

---

[86] Lowe and Yasuhara, *Origins.*   [87] Ibid.

religious persuasions. Other forms of sophisticated knowledge, not least in the natural sciences and technology, developed in various types of state-run institutes.[88]

Examples from older Asian and European history indicate that numerous institutions of higher learning existed long before the emergence of the university in the high mediaeval Christian West. At the same time, it is obvious that the university as an institution of knowledge had its own distinctive features. Its fundamental mission was to transmit older truths. Research – in its present meaning of actively and systematically generating new, science-based knowledge – did not become a key concern of the university until the nineteenth century. Instead, mediaeval academic teachers essentially administered, handed down, and interpreted Classical or Christian authorities. This was accomplished mainly through lectures, but also through disputations, in both cases using Latin as a lingua franca. The raison d'être of the university was to provide advanced studies for future priests, lawyers, physicians, and civil servants based on the worldview of mediaeval culture.[89]

In a wider perspective, the mediaeval university turned out to be an extraordinarily vital institution that was able to survive under various societal systems. Referring back to the discussion of knowledge circulation, it is interesting to investigate how this model of advanced knowledge adapted to new realities when transferred to other parts of the world. When an institution is established in a new context it can be modelled to various degrees on an older pattern, but local circumstances always have an impact, and the institution may acquire other functions, structures, and tasks. For example, Spanish colonisers were the first and most active in founding universities on the American continents in the sixteenth century. Inspiration came mainly from the Spanish academic tradition, especially the University of Salamanca. Early on, the Spanish academic offensive in Latin America was interwoven with the greater Christian mission, and ecclesiastical orders usually played an important role at various kinds of educational institutions. It was not uncommon for a seminary or monastery to develop into a university, often maintaining its strong ecclesiastical character. This was the case for the first university established in the New World, in Santo Domingo in 1538 in present-day Dominican Republic. In 1551, the Spanish crown sanctioned founding universities in Lima and Mexico City.[90]

Consequently, by combining global and knowledge history, it is possible to reinterpret the history of the university and distance it from a Eurocentric norm. Similarly, other research into the history of knowledge can open up new

---

[88] Ibid.   [89] Rüegg and Ridder-Symoens, *History.*   [90] Ridder-Symoens, *History.*

perspectives on the history of knowledge institutions. Sebastian Felten and Christine von Oertzen have, in a special issue of the *Journal for the History of Knowledge*, used the concept of *bureaucratic knowledge* for this purpose. They define bureaucracies as 'socio-material structures in perpetual motion, which constantly adapt their procedures to meet shifting goals as they regulate state, economic, or religious affairs'. With this definition, Felten and von Oertzen challenge a modern understanding of bureaucracy closely linked to Max Weber, in order to be able to instead study and compare such things as churches, businesses, and states from different periods and cultures. They focus on the epistemic dimensions and knowledge practices of bureaucracies, in order to 'recover actors' ways of organizing the social and material worlds'.[91]

This special issue also contains several empirical contributions that deal with bureaucratic knowledge or bureaucracies of knowledge. Harun Küçük writes about the practices of knowledge developed for taxing the population of the Ottoman Empire in the seventeenth century. Sixiang Wang analyses how Korea in the early modern era built up a corps of translators and interpreters in the service of diplomacy. Anna Echterhölter investigates how German academics and bureaucrats mapped indigenous legal traditions in the colony of German New Guinea in the decades around 1900.[92]

Inspired by this type of research, it is possible to study the university as an institution of knowledge based on new approaches. Not least can the university's administrative system, organisational form, and production of knowledge be linked to sweeping societal changes in the surrounding world. This is true of the processes of early modern state formation, of the Sovietisation of Russian universities after 1917, of the Europeanisation of the European universities since the 1980s, and of numerous other processes where institutions of knowledge have undergone significant changes.

In summary, in this section, we have introduced a few key concepts from the history of knowledge and demonstrated how they may be used. We are well aware that this focus means that we have not been able to draw attention to other fruitful concepts and perspectives in the field. For example, practical knowledge or 'know-how' has been studied by both Pamela H. Smith and Dagmar Schäfer.[93] Other historians, including Joshua Ehrlich, have taken an interest in the politics of knowledge and the suppression of knowledge.[94] Still others, such as Ann Blair, have analysed how knowledge scarcity and knowledge glut have been dealt with in different historical contexts.[95]

---

[91] Felten and Oertzen, 'Bureaucracy', 2.

[92] Küçük, 'Bureaucratic'; Wang, 'Chosŏn's'; Echterhölter, 'Shells'.

[93] Smith, *Body*; Schäfer, *Crafting*.   [94] Ehrlich, *East India*.   [95] Blair, *Too*.

In this small Element, we cannot delve deeply into all the exciting subdivisions of the history of knowledge. In the following section, we will instead be more specific, and provide examples from our own research of how the history of knowledge can be conducted.

3 Knowledge in Circulation: Society and People's Lives

3.1 Introduction

As we have seen, the history of knowledge can be written in many different ways and via various specialisations. The field is open and invites researchers from different backgrounds and with different interests. At the same time, it cannot simply be a general meeting place for sundry researchers in the humanities who are interested in knowledge; if it were, it would risk becoming far too diffuse, lacking in identity. Instead, we feel that the field has and should have the capacity to generate research. It has doubtlessly been so for us.

In this section, we provide more tangible and empirically based examples of precisely what a knowledge-historical perspective might entail, and how it can give rise to new productive research. Above all, we would like to illustrate what sets knowledge-historical investigations apart from those of the history of culture, education, or science.

Our analytical point of departure is the circulation of knowledge, that is, one of the most popular concepts in the history of knowledge. We focus on two kinds of circulation. First, we take up what we call the societal circulation of knowledge. The starting point is, as was made clear in the previous section, that knowledge is studied as a broader societal phenomenon with a not insignificant social reach and importance. Second, we provide examples of how the circulation of knowledge shaped people's lives. This means that knowledge in various ways impacted the trajectories of the lives of individuals and influenced their relationships to existence at large. Concretely, this could manifest itself as follows: acquired knowledge could influence the ideas, convictions, and identities of particular individuals, but skills and abilities picked up could also form the foundations of their professional paths and careers. In addition, knowledge could in diverse ways encourage action and cause people to maintain, adjust, or change habits, behaviours, or lifestyles.[96]

In the following, we will demonstrate how knowledge circulation can manifest itself. Our examples are drawn from three research fields where we have been active in recent years: environmental history, the history of the humanities, and the history of knowledge of shareholding. As researchers, we have dealt

---

[96] Östling and Larsson Heidenblad, 'Fulfilling'.

mainly with modern history in the Western world, and this specialisation is reflected in the historical examples we cite. At the same time, our goal is for these specific cases to illustrate more general points and problems in the history of knowledge. We begin each exemplification with circulation in society, and then move on to knowledge in people's lives. It soon becomes obvious that it is often difficult to completely separate these two approaches: they tend to interact with each other, and at times are two sides of the same coin.

3.1.1 The Breakthrough of Environmental Issues

On 22 April 1970, Fifth Avenue in New York changed its appearance. Instead of honking taxicabs and fuming exhaust pipes the street was, for one day, filled with people. The reason was the first nation-wide Earth Day celebration. People gathered in streets and sports arenas, schools and campuses. It is estimated that in total twenty million Americans participated in the event. Earth Day became one of the greatest political manifestations of its time. Neither the protests against the Vietnam War nor the various activities of the civil rights movement brought together as many people on a single occasion as did the Earth Day celebrations.

Earth Day was organised as a so-called teach-in, a semi-academic format that had emerged in the 1960s. The day's activities were primarily speeches, seminars, workshops, and panel discussions. Simultaneously, there were demonstrations and actions to clean up litter. In other words, Earth Day was not one single thing but many things linked together. The aim was to educate people and make them more aware of the global environmental crisis, but also to encourage political action.

The initiator of Earth Day was Gaylord Nelson, a Democratic Senator from Wisconsin. In the 1960s, he had developed an active commitment to environmental issues, and had attempted, through political action, to introduce stricter laws in various areas. His attempts had, however, been fruitless. It proved difficult to convince other politicians of the seriousness of the situation. Environmental issues did not play a particularly significant role in the presidential election of 1968. But when Nelson himself spoke to people, he noticed that the environment engendered a deep commitment, especially among college students. This gave him the idea of a nation-wide teach-in that could channel the burgeoning interest and build public opinion that other politicians could not ignore. Therefore, he assembled a team of young persons from various student movements who had experience in organising. In November 1969, the celebration of Earth Day was announced for 22 April 1970.

In the following months, preparatory work developed into a national grass roots movement. All across the United States, a multitude of small independent organising committees were established. They tackled issues that were important locally and framed these in a global perspective. Approximately 1,500 colleges and 10,000 secondary schools arranged teach-ins. The day after the celebration, the picture of the crowds in Fifth Avenue graced the front page of the *New York Times*: 'Millions Join Earth Day Observances across the Nation' was the headline. In this way, environmental issues had a significant societal breakthrough in the United States.[97]

In the years around 1970, there were similar breakthroughs in many other parts of the world. Knowledge that had long engaged only small groups of people rapidly became the concern of entire societies. Historians speak of this as *the environmental turn*. In knowledge-historical research, this has become a representative example of what is meant by the societal circulation of knowledge and a societal breakthrough of knowledge. What was difficult to know in 1966 was difficult *not* to know in 1971. How did this happen? What were the reasons for it? Why did it happen at this precise point in time, and what were the consequences?[98]

This type of issue is at the centre of studies of the societal circulation of knowledge. Research here is concerned with the social relevance, reach, preconditions, and transformation of various kinds of knowledge, unlike in other specialisations, where greater emphasis is placed on the origins and formation of knowledge. From this latter perspective, the years around 1970 are not particularly decisive, because the knowledge in circulation was, in form and content, neither new nor original. From a history of ideas perspective, it is rather the late 1940s that are key to the birth of modern environmental awareness. This is when a new understanding was established concerning how human beings, nature, the world, and the future are connected. The very concept of the environment acquired new meaning. Previously, 'the environment' had denoted external circumstances that affected human beings. Now use of the term began to indicate how human actions transformed the world. Human beings were seen as a force of nature and as a danger to themselves.

Two important works from this time are Fairfield Osborn's *Our Plundered Planet* and William Vogt's *Road to Survival*. Both were published in the United States in 1948 and both became international bestsellers. They emphasised that 'by excessive breeding and abuse of the land mankind has backed itself into an ecological trap'. In order to avoid global collapse drastic measures were required, and a reorientation of our relationship to the world in which we live.

---

[97] Rome, *Genius.*   [98] Larsson Heidenblad, *Environmental.*

We could no longer 'believe valid our assumption that we live in independence', but instead needed to thoroughly learn of 'our dependence upon the earth and the riches with which it sustains us'.[99]

Neither Vogt nor Osborn worked covertly. They took positions in public life and attracted considerable attention. It is easy to find quotes in their books that are similar, if not identical, to what was said on Earth Day in 1970. At the same time, the books did not engender a profound and lasting commitment among politicians or the public when they were published. In the following years, knowledge concerning a global environmental crisis circulated primarily in small elite groups, such as the conference *Man's Role in Changing the Face of the Earth*, held at Princeton in June 1955. There, seventy-three researchers from around the world gathered to discuss global challenges faced by humanity. At this type of meeting, foundations were laid for international scientific ventures like the International Geophysical Year of 1957–1958. In its wake, the concept of *environmental sciences* was coined c. 1960.[100]

From a broader societal perspective, scientific development regarding this issue was still virtually imperceptible. The only global threat that engaged larger groups of people in the late 1950s and early 1960s was the threat of nuclear annihilation. Schoolchildren learned how to shelter under their desks, social debaters raised their voices, and concerned scientists warned of the dangers of radiation. In many Western countries, people gathered to participate in peace marches and to demand disarmament. The culmination was the Cuban Missile Crisis of 1962. However, the following year the so-called Partial Test Ban Treaty was signed. This was followed by a long period of high-level political detente and declining grass roots involvement with these issues.[101]

Parallel to this, however, knowledge about a looming environmental crisis reached wider circles. Decisive here was Rachel Carson's book *Silent Spring* (1962) that pointed out the dangers of chemical pesticides such as DDT. She warned that birdsong would fall silent and that human DNA risked degrading. Carson's book occasioned a massive debate in the United States between biologists and nature conservation interests on the one hand, and chemists and representatives of the chemical industry on the other. But politicians also began to tackle the biocide issue. President John F. Kennedy appointed a science commission to clarify the dangers of the situation. In May 1963, it presented its report indicating great uncertainty about the unforeseen consequences that a continued use of DDT might have. Discovering the true situation required

[99] Vogt, *Road*, 284 and 286.   [100] Warde, *Environment*.   [101] Boyer, *Bomb's*.

more research. This prompted rich countries such as the United States and Sweden to launch major new research efforts in the environmental field.[102]

The Swedish initiative, the 1964 government inquiry on nature resources, was to be especially important for global developments. The inquiry assembled experts in the natural sciences, who worked in close collaboration with politicians and the armed forces. Within the framework of the inquiry, pioneering discoveries were made concerning environmental hazards such as mercury and acid rain. The latter was to have far-reaching consequences. The Swedish public became aware of the threat in October 1967, and it immediately impacted the national environmental debate. It became clear that pollution and emissions could not be reduced to local problems. Since environmental toxins knew no borders, increased international co-operation was needed to deal with them. Shortly thereafter, Swedish diplomats put these issues on the global political agenda. This led to the first United Nations conference on the human environment in June 1972 in Stockholm. Politicians, researchers, and environmental activists from around the world gathered in the city's streets and squares.[103]

But what happened to the knowledge about a global environmental crisis when it began to circulate in society? Was it perceived and handled in the same way in 1971 as in 1967? No, knowledge-historical studies show that there were major changes over these years. In the early breakthrough phase there was considerable consensus concerning this issue. In the United States, the environment was an area that Democrats and Republicans could agree on. They jointly supported stricter environmental laws and the establishment of the Environmental Protection Agency. Not until later did the environment become a polarising party-political issue.[104]

The same pattern can be seen in Sweden, where the chemist Hans Palmstierna, through his 1967 book *Plundring, svält, förgiftning* (Plunder, starvation, poisoning), initially functioned as a unifying persona. His was a voice that was listened to in all camps, and through his broad network of contacts in science, politics, and mass media, he soon exerted an enormous influence. Via the various organisations of the labour movement, he developed study circles, TV programmes, and campaigns intended to make young people more environmentally aware.

This was possible because in the breakthrough phase environmental issues were neither clearly left nor right. They were thought to be purely a matter of knowledge. After more and better studies, and with a more enlightened opinion, society would take action. When this began to happen, however, numerous conflicts of interest emerged. How should environmental values be balanced

---

[102] Cross, 'Silent'.   [103] Larsson Heidenblad, *Environmental*.   [104] Coodley, *Green*.

against jobs and economic growth? Should the state plan and regulate, or could problems be better solved by a self-regulating business community and market forces? The boundaries between knowledge and opinion, science and ideology, were completely different before, during, and after the societal breakthrough of knowledge.

Furthermore, the emergence of a number of new environmental movements changed the dynamics of the debate. The people within these movements were young radicals who wanted to make big, rapid changes, creating tension between them and an older tradition of nature conservation, which traditionally had a conservative bias. The new environmental movements were skilful in gaining media attention through demonstrations and direct action.[105]

Nevertheless, there is a danger in focusing unilaterally on what was written, said, and done in public. The waves of the debate are one thing, working practically and long term for change is something else. The latter can happen without providing headlines, for instance by establishing educational courses, creating new professions, or working for change in municipalities and companies.

Once the breakthrough of environmental issues has occurred at a societal level, it is not difficult to find ideas for further research. However, here it is important to find a balance between studying a specific society, such as Sweden or the United States, and adopting a broader international view. After all, modern environmental awareness is, as demonstrated by environmental historians Ramachandra Guha and Joachim Radkau, a global phenomenon. It engendered new ways of relating to concepts such as *humanity* and *the planet*.[106]

In this context, the first photographs of Earth from space, taken from lunar orbit in 1968 by the crew of Apollo 8, play a special role. The most famous of these, 'Earthrise', shows how the Earth rises above the lifeless landscape of the moon. Today it is still one of the most widely disseminated and reproduced photographs in the world. A radical cultural power for change was attributed to the Apollo pictures already by their contemporaries. These photos, it was thought, provided an overview of the planet that enabled people see their existence in a completely new way. Historian Robert Poole feels that 'Earthrise' gave people an image to think with.[107]

But were the photographs actually decisive for the breakthrough of environmental issues? Can images have such great significance? It is difficult to provide a firm answer to that question. After all, there is a long history of imagining Earth as seen from space. This thought experiment can be found already in

---

[105] Larsson Heidenblad, *Environmental.*   [106] Guha, *Environmentalism*; Radkau, *Age.*
[107] Poole, *Earthrise.*

classical writers such as Cicero and Seneca. What is emphasised there is the insignificance of human life. Adopting a cosmic perspective urges people to feel humility in the face of their existence. The same ideas can be found in popular science and science fiction novels from the 1950s. Nevertheless, it is clear that the actual photographs of Earth from space played a major role in the environmental turn. Earth Day would hardly have been celebrated without them.

3.1.2 Environmental Knowledge in People's Lives

In the summer of 1971, eleven-year-old Mats Lidström from Gothenburg wrote a letter to Hans Palmstierna, the best-known environmental debater in Sweden. Lidström had recently read a story about environmentalism to which Palmstierna had contributed. The story had had a profound effect on him. 'Is our little Tellus really in such dire straits?' he wondered. Lidström wrote that it was awful that there were people who destroyed the environment only to make money. 'They ought to be taught a real lesson', he felt, for everything they did to those who had 'just been born'. It was now his generation that would be forced to 'fight against humanity's possible destruction and [for its] existence'.

To learn more about environmental problems, the boy had bought Palmstierna's book *Plundring, svält, förgiftning*. He found it incredibly interesting and informative, but also depressing. 'How can anybody be happy in this society?' he asked. He had taken the book to school several times to read aloud from it. Not many of his classmates had wanted to listen. 'And that is of course an example of why the world looks the way it does', he observed. He thought of becoming in the future 'someone who works with the environment'.

Palmstierna answered the boy quickly, amiably, and comprehensively. He agreed that money and a desire for profit far too often controlled the way of the world. 'Like you I am convinced', he continued 'that you and others born in the fifties and sixties will pay dearly for the mistakes made by my generation and the generations immediately before mine'. Continued environmental destruction had to be stopped. Humans had to be protected from themselves. 'Long term this becomes a question of our survival, if we do not improve'.

This correspondence provides an insight into how knowledge about an environmental crisis intruded in people's lives in Sweden in the early 1970s. It shows that knowledge not only circulated among the public and was a concern for society's elites. It could also awaken thoughts in an eleven-year-old schoolboy. What would the world be like when he grew up? What challenges awaited him and his classmates? Was the environmental crisis truly a threat to the survival of humanity?

A few years earlier, a pre-teen's worries about the future would hardly have been formulated in this way. In the mid-1960s, few people warned of humanity's being on the verge of a global environmental crisis. But over a few years in the late 1960s, a radical change occurred – a societal breakthrough of knowledge. And this had consequences for many people. They began to think new thoughts and do new things. Among the younger generation, there were those who demonstrated against environmental destruction, joined established environmental organisations, or started their own environmental groups. Others turned their backs on the big city and civilisation and moved to the countryside to live a simpler life – perhaps even attempting to become self-sufficient.[108]

How this new commitment manifested itself in people's everyday lives is an important knowledge-historical question. By exploring this, we can analyse what a societal knowledge breakthrough involves. What happens to people who become environmentally aware? Do they begin to act in new ways? Is knowledge transformed by encounters with everyday life? Questions such as these can be posed broadly, both to those who at beginning of the 1970s made radical life changes and to those who did not. What were the actual relationships among knowledge, action, everyday life, and politics?

One way to approach this issue with respect to Sweden is to examine Hans Palmstierna's voluminous private correspondence. After his big breakthrough in the autumn of 1967, people with different backgrounds and professions wrote to him from across the country. Among these were politicians and intellectuals, students and old age pensioners, bank directors and priests, doctors and schoolchildren. Overall, these letters provide insights into what people thought and did when they became aware of environmental issues, and how their commitment developed over time.

One of the earliest letters from the general public was written by Sören Gunnarsson in October 1967. He stated that Palmstierna's newspaper articles had 'meant a great deal to me and stimulated my thoughts about the serious problems you write about'. Gunnarsson observed that the debate on 'pollution and the exploitation of the earth' had intensified during the previous year. He expressed increasing uneasiness and worry about 'the ruthlessness by which big industries are destroying future opportunities for life'. Troubled, he turned to Palmstierna for information and advice. What was being done by those in authority? How did people act who realised that humanity was threatened? What could a layman do other than read the writings of scientists?

Palmstierna answered in detail and related how he had tried to work for change within and through the Social Democratic party, which had dominated

---

[108] Larsson Heidenblad, *Environmental*.

Swedish politics since the 1930s. He agreed with Gunnarsson's criticism of an 'egotistical desire for profit', and pointed out that an ecological committee had been formed within the natural sciences. The two men would continue to correspond with each other over the coming months. Together they made plans for the future about creating a special interest group or even starting a popular movement. 'The time has come for this', wrote Palmstierna. He was buoyed by the success of his book and his co-operation with various organisations, among these a large insurance company. He and this insurance company jointly created the campaign 'Front against Environmental Destruction', one of the aims of which was awakening young people's commitment and transforming them into well-educated environmentalists. Through this campaign, we can see how the growing commitment was channelled.

The largest groups that turned to Palmstierna in these years were upper secondary school and university students. Many of these took initiatives of their own. They organised lectures, wrote articles, started educational courses, and arranged exhibitions. Palmstierna himself was happy to assist them. He saw students as a key group for creating change. In a few years, they would be the ones sitting in decision-making positions in municipalities and companies. The future belonged to them.[109]

Whether Senator Gaylord Nelson of Wisconsin thought in terms of similar long-term goals is unclear, but Earth Day filled such a function. This gives knowledge historians an opportunity to study how people's lives are affected and shaped by a societal breakthrough of knowledge, that is, by identifying actors and following them over the course of decades. This is what environmental historian Adam Rome did in his study *The Genius of Earth Day*, which is about the prelude to, implementation of, and long-term consequences of the first Earth Day celebration. He argues that Earth Day was much more than an event of the moment. It had long-term effects that can hardly be overestimated.

In 1969, there was no organised environmental movement in the United States. Certainly, knowledge about an environmental crisis did circulate in the public sphere, including through controversial books like Barry Commoner's *Science and Survival* (1966) and *The Population Bomb* (1968) by Paul and Anne Howland Ehrlich. But the step from knowledge to political activism was not obvious. Here, Earth Day functioned as a catalyst. Both its planning and implementation gave young people experience, networks, and organisational practice. According to Rome, Earth Day created 'the first green generation'.

One of these people was Nancy Pearlman. She was one of the organisers of Earth Day at the University of California, Los Angeles (UCLA). In this way, she

---

[109] Ibid.

met older women who had long worked with specific nature conservation issues. She herself wanted to implement a more comprehensive approach to environmental issues, and for this reason in 1972 she founded the Ecology Center of Southern California. She began to publish a newsletter, and throughout the 1970s combined environmental activism and frequent media appearances with her career as a teacher. In 1977, she was offered the opportunity to launch her own radio show: 'Environmental Directions', which is still being broadcast (at the time of writing, about 2,300 programmes have been recorded).

Another person was Karim Ahmed, who arrived at the University of Minnesota from Pakistan in 1960. He wished to become a natural scientist and make major discoveries. Politics did not interest him in the least. But towards the end of the 1960s, he became actively engaged with the issue of Vietnam. He organised demonstrations and went on hunger strikes. At the same time, he commenced postgraduate studies in biochemistry and became involved in the organisation of Earth Day. As with Nancy Pearlman, this marked the beginning of lifelong environmental activism. Instead of a traditional researcher Ahmed became, through his work in different environmental organisations, a spokesman for other people's research.[110]

Similar events took place at our own Department of History in Lund. Here Professor Birgitta Odén became actively involved with environmental issues in the 1960s, in part because her younger brother Svante Odén was the person who identified the environmental dangers of acid rain. She redirected her research interests from sixteenth-century government finances to modern industrial society's relationship to the environment and natural resources. Around 1970, she encouraged students to start new research projects and managed to form a research group dealing with environmental history. One of its members, Lars J. Lundgren, published his thesis in 1974 and afterwards ended up working for the Swedish Environmental Protection Agency. He combined this with writing about environmental history. For instance, his book *Acid Rain on the Agenda* presents a detailed description of how acid rain became a media and political issue.[111]

But must knowledge-historical studies of the environment in people's lives focus on specific actors and their life stories? No, other approaches are available for those who do not want historiography to become too biographical and particular. One is focusing on broad social phenomena and activities that at a certain point in time directly or indirectly concern everyone in society. In the environmental arena one can, for instance, imagine doing studies on bottle

---

[110] Rome, *Genius*.   [111] Larsson Heidenblad, 'Environmental'; Lundgren, *Acid*.

deposits, waste separation, or environmental labelling of products. All these things are common today, but did not exist in the mid-1960s. When, how, and where did these systems develop? What was done to make people change their habitual behaviours?

If we move further forward in time, we can also study the emergence, breakthrough, and development of the issue of climate change. Today this issue intrudes directly in many people's lives. It influences their choices of transport, diet, and consumption. But when did this occur? How did it happen? These questions are well suited for knowledge-historical studies that put an emphasis on how knowledge circulates and is used – rather than how it is created.

The great media breakthrough of the climate change issue occurred in the autumn of 2006. At a global level, former American Vice-President Al Gore's film *An Inconvenient Truth* was especially important. But many forces contributed, and in Swedish media there was during the breakthrough phase a strong focus on what an individual could do. In the tabloid *Aftonbladet*, a climate change appeal to 'Do something now!' was launched, which urged readers to begin to change their personal behaviours. The newspaper wanted to show that individuals could counteract climate change and put pressure on politicians to act, for instance by making a climate change pledge to use public transport more often or to replace old lightbulbs with low-energy variants. This appeal collected over 300,000 signatures and was followed up by articles about people who chose to make lifestyle changes because of the climate crisis.[112]

But it was not mainly in the public sphere that efforts of this type took place. For this reason, historians of knowledge would be wise to direct their attention to other locations where people's lives are lived and formed, such as schools and places of work. Here, one can study developments in curricula and teaching materials, arrangements concerning continuing education days, and the work done on environmental certification and climate policies. This type of contemporary phenomena and action for change are not obviously historicised. The focus when it comes to climate and environmental issues often lies in creating an alternative future. But all of these practices are historical. They are a part of a longer environmental and knowledge history. If we want to create a sustainable society, we would be wise to take advantage of people's experiences from the more than fifty years that have passed since environmental knowledge began to intervene in their lives.

---

[112] Larsson Heidenblad, *Vårt.*

3.1.3 The Humanities in the Public Sphere

Humanists have long written their own history. Biographical or discipline-historical accounts have long dominated, where prominent figures from the past or developments in a particular subject were central. However, sophisticated methods and tools of analysis – long used to write the history of medicine, technology, and natural science – were conspicuous by their absence in studies of the humanities. However, as pointed out in our introduction, a vitalisation has taken place in the last few years, and the history of the humanities has emerged as an independent field.[113]

One new and fruitful way of analysing the past of the humanities is to apply a knowledge-historical perspective. Researchers can then zoom out from the world of learning and its institutions, and instead illuminate the importance of humanistic knowledge for society at large. This can be done by studying how humanists have functioned as knowledge actors in the public sphere, thereby using knowledge circulation as an analytic framework.[114]

One way of concretising the study of circulation is by focusing on the public knowledge arenas where it took place. A knowledge arena is, as pointed out in the previous section, a place that provides an opportunity and sets boundaries for the circulation of knowledge, a kind of meeting place or venue for a certain kind of knowledge actors and certain types of audience. Below, we exemplify this with three major media knowledge arenas in the Western European public sphere – the press, broadcast media, and non-fiction paperback books – and the humanists active there.[115]

Throughout the twentieth century, the press was a central forum for academic outreach, not least for philosophers, historians, literary scholars, and other humanists, who wrote for newspaper culture pages and participated in public debates. In many cases, there were close personal links between newspaper editorial offices and leading publicists on the one hand, and professors and various university teachers on the other. This created a symbiotic relationship that supplied an important precondition for the circulation of knowledge.

West Germany can serve as an example. In the newspaper landscape that emerged following World War II, writers, intellectuals, and researchers in the humanities began to appear on the culture pages (*Feuilleton*). *Frankfurter Allgemeine Zeitung*, for instance, was a leading liberal-conservative newspaper in the public sphere at the time, and among its contributors were critics, authors, and researchers with strong connections to the academic humanities. This was

---

[113] Bod et al., 'New Field'.
[114] Hammar and Östling, 'Circulation'; Östling, Jansson, and Svensson, 'Public Arenas'.
[115] Ibid.; Östling, 'Circulation, Arenas'.

true not least for several influential editors, who themselves wrote longer articles while simultaneously ordering material, editing texts, and maintaining contacts with the world of the humanities. Not unexpectedly, the newspaper's culture pages offered much space to the humanities in the form of book reviews of non-fiction literature and essays on philosophical, historical, and aesthetic subjects. Occasionally, a special section devoted considerable attention to new research in the humanities. On the whole, the culture pages of *FAZ* can be regarded as a knowledge arena where the humanities of the post-war years held a prominent position.[116]

The humanist culture of learning that manifested itself on the culture pages of *FAZ* had counterparts in other countries. One of Sweden's leading newspapers, *Svenska Dagbladet*, had published a daily essay since 1918. This special section was called 'Under strecket' (Below the line) and was intended as a neutral forum for discussing cultural or scientific questions of interest to the educated general public, presented in a manner accessible to everyone. Every conceivable subject – literary, artistic, scientific, historical, social, economic – was open for discussion, but on examination of the articles, a clear pattern emerges. In the post-war years, this was an important arena for humanists. Historians and literary scholars in particular played important roles, frequently providing publicity for the academic humanities in one of Sweden's largest dailies.[117]

Other Western European newspapers and periodicals were also important knowledge arenas in the post-war years, functioning as meeting places for academic researchers and a wide circle of readers. National variations were sometimes considerable, but on the whole, the press was exceptionally important for the links between the university and the public sphere.

Another example of the place of the humanities in post-war society can be found in radio and television. These offered larger public knowledge arenas for academics. Radio was introduced in the interwar years and became an important forum for lectures on popular science. In many Western European countries, serious, well-read contributors with strong cultural capital were recruited for radio. These were mainly academics, who then contributed to the hiring of even more academics. The result was that a significant portion of the programme staff in the early post-war era had an academic education, often with a degree in the humanities. The BBC, which was the primary role model for most Western European radio companies, acquired many of their staff from Oxford or Cambridge. At least prior to the 1960s these linguists, historians, and classicists functioned as knowledge actors responsible for lectures, popular education, and

---

[116] Schildt, *Medien-Intellektuelle*; Hoeres, *Zeitung*.
[117] Östling, Jansson, and Svensson Stringberg, *Humanister*.

cultural transmission, not seldom as managers or hosts. Their personal experience of acquiring knowledge at a high level in the humanities meant that they could function as guarantors of high-quality content. They also ensured a continuing active connection between broadcast media on the one hand and the university on the other.[118]

As the 1960s replaced the 1950s, new winds began to blow in many Western European countries. The 'age of TV' was at hand, the beginning of a sweeping cultural revolution. The breakthrough of television coincided with and accelerated the liberalisation of society and a questioning of traditional authorities, including the university and established media. At the same time, entertainment became an increasingly important element in broadcast media. This contributed to the advancement of new programmes and expressions. All these changes had an impact on the preconditions for the circulation of knowledge in the public sphere.[119]

In this new media landscape, there were a number of distinct knowledge arenas where academics appeared. One example can be taken from Sweden. In September 1962 the first episode of what was to become one of the most popular TV shows of the decade was broadcast, *Fråga Lund* (Ask Lund). Each week six academics from Lund University assembled to answer questions from the general public. This learned panel was led by Jan-Öjvind Swahn, a docent (reader) in folkloristics, and included five other men – a philologist, a physicist, a medical researcher, an entomologist, and a historian.[120]

From a knowledge-historical perspective, it is particularly interesting to note what this arena tells us about the place of the humanities in post-war society. Not everything discussed in the programme belonged in the humanities, but it is clear that this field of knowledge had a strong and obvious position in public service television in the 1960s. Many questions answered in the popular programme had a humanistic dimension, and three of the six original learned men were readers or professors in subjects in the humanities. What was manifested in *Fråga Lund* was a kind of culture of learning, and in that culture the humanities were a stable feature. It is indeed difficult to imagine this culture without the obvious inclusion of history, languages, and ideas as essential elements.[121]

A third arena of knowledge in the post-war public sphere that was of great importance for humanists was the non-fiction paperback book. Like broadcast media, the book market had well-established traditions for the transmission of knowledge, but there was also a demand for renewal.

---

[118] Englom, *Radio- och TV-folket.*   [119] Schildt and Siegfried, *Deutsche.*
[120] Östling, Jansson, and Svensson Stringberg, *Humanister.*   [121] Ibid.

The paperback had its heyday in the late 1950s and for two decades thereafter. The paperback format itself existed already in the interwar years, for instance with publishers such as Penguin in the United Kingdom and Pocket Books in the United States, but what has been called *the paperback revolution* took place in the 1960s. This is when the paperback became a medium representative of its time for the advanced discussion of ideas and the transmission of knowledge. Not only larger, well-established publishers but also their smaller, alternative counterparts invested heavily in publishing paperbacks. The low price and convenient format made it possible to sell these books in kiosks, railway stations, and regular bookshops. Not least a younger circle of readers was attracted to paperbacks, which became an important feature of the left-wing radical movements of the late 1960s and early 1970s.[122]

In most Western European countries, non-fiction paperbacks focused on popular science and were often published in special book series. For example, in West Germany the Rowohlt German Encyclopaedia (*rowohlts deutsche enzyklopädie*, abbreviated *rde*) became a household term. Over four hundred titles were published in this series of paperbacks, beginning in the late 1950s. These books encompassed a wide register of knowledge, but focused on the humanities. Several were written by the most renowned researchers of the time, and many sold in large quantities.[123] In Sweden, the Aldus series (published by the leading publisher Bonniers) played a similar role. This was an exclusively non-fiction book series focusing on advanced popular science. Beginning in 1957, 450 titles by both Swedish and international writers were published over the following two decades. Many of these writers were prominent humanists.[124]

These three examples – the culture pages of the press, the popular education programmes of broadcast media, and non-fiction paperbacks – were all important as knowledge arenas for humanists of the post-war era. Being active in the public sphere was an obvious component of the professional identity of many of these researchers; indeed, in many cases it was difficult to separate their scholarly from their public personae.

By adopting a knowledge-historical perspective, it is thus possible to write a somewhat different history about the humanities of the post-war era. It is no longer a story about how an old, well-established field of knowledge was gradually marginalised and lost its influence to the natural and social sciences. Instead, we see how humanists were central to culture, the media, and the discussion of ideas in post-war society. In this manner, the history of knowledge can reveal new understandings and contribute to reinterpretations.

---

[122] Mercer, 'Paperback'.   [123] Döring, Lewandowski, and Oels, *Rowohlts.*
[124] Östling, Jansson, and Svensson Stringberg, *Humanister.*

3.1.4 The Humanities in People's Lives

Just as was the case with the breakthrough of the environmental issue mentioned earlier, we cannot simply concentrate on the public sphere if we are to understand the more prominent place and deeper meaning of knowledge in modern society. Humanistic knowledge did not just circulate in a number of media arenas and was not merely a concern for the intellectual and scholarly groups of the time. Instead, the humanities also intervened in people's lives and shaped their careers, identities, and lifestyles. A broad knowledge-historical perspective may enable us to see how this happened.

The aim of an education in the humanities at upper secondary or university level has long been to enable students to develop as people and citizens, and additionally – like in so many other types of education – to prepare them for professional life. Through studies of languages, history, literature, or other humanistic subjects, a foundation of knowledge is established for a number of professions.

In an investigation of Australia of the interwar period, Tamson Pietsch and Gabrielle Kemmis show how the careers of students from the humanities could develop. They refute a common belief that people with degrees in the humanities almost exclusively became teachers. Instead they demonstrate, using digital historical tools, that humanists could be found in a number of society's sectors, among these the civil service, the judicial system, politics, and the church, as well as business, agriculture, and the health services. In addition, the authors show that studies in the humanities promoted geographical and social mobility. After an education in Sydney or Perth, a humanist could get a job as a librarian in a medium-size city in Queensland, or as an upper secondary school teacher in Tasmania.[125]

A more general insight is that humanities alumni can be seen as a form of embodied knowledge. For a few years in their youth, they immersed themselves in Latin, art history, or practical philosophy, which gave them skills and abilities employed later in their professional lives. Additionally, they functioned as bearers of knowledge, ambassadors of academic knowledge in different segments of society. With respect to Norway, Fredrik Thue has claimed that the humanities had a circuit of their own. After having studied in Oslo or Bergen, philologists and historians were employed in smaller towns such as Hamar or Ålesund and were there able to transmit their knowledge and values in classrooms, museums, and local newspapers. University professors, who not seldom had worked as upper secondary school teachers before acquiring a desirable academic job, functioned as a kind of principal for the nation. The same pattern

---

[125] Pietsch and Kemmis, 'Careers'.

can be identified in other countries. In the decades following World War II, an increasingly clearer role as a researcher crystallised, and many who had ambitions for an academic career remained in the universities. As a consequence, the traditional circuit of knowledge weakened, and the distance increased between the university on the one hand, and upper secondary schools, museums, and cultural institutions on the other.[126]

However, humanistic improvement was not just something that shaped people's careers; it could also influence identities. One example can be taken from the twentieth-century Christian cultural sphere in Western Europe. Even in relatively secularised countries, such as the United Kingdom and the Scandinavian countries, there was a lively publication of Christian books and periodicals via which theological and humanistic research circulated. Special publishing companies, periodicals, and institutions supported this Christian segment of the public sphere. To many key people in this sphere – authors, translators, critics, priests – their humanistic educational background was something that also shaped them as people and provided a foundation for their philosophies of life. Using philosophy, history, or literature, they explored reality and navigated existence.[127]

Nor were the humanities reserved for intellectual or cultural elites. For instance, broader social groups could also partake of the history and literature of antiquity, turning to these as a source of self-knowledge, learning, escapism, or recreation. In a comprehensive examination of the significance of classical antiquity for the British and Irish working classes from the seventeenth century to World War II, Edith Hall and Henry Stead refute the thesis that the proletarian cultures were a 'Classics-Free Zone'. Instead they provide numerous examples of how intensely present Graeco-Roman antiquity was in the cultural and educational activities of the working classes, in everything from theatre performances and cheap books to museum exhibitions and popular science magazines.[128]

In a completely different way, the humanities could also underpin ideological ideas or be part of people's political aspirations. Studies have shown how German historians in the 1930s and 1940s actively participated in several Nazi projects. Some people did this from opportunism, others from political or moral convictions. A number of researchers, for example, contributed to so-called Western studies (*Westforschung*), and one of Hitler's arguments for annexing Belgium in World War II was based on studies of the German heritage in Wallonia carried out by these historians. The subject of history thus provided

---

[126] Thue and Helsvig, *Universitetet.*

[127] Östling, Jansson, and Svensson Stringberg, *Humanister.*   [128] Hall and Stead, *People's.*

scholarly legitimacy to expansive racial politics.[129] In a similar manner, historians in so-called Eastern studies (*Ostforschung*) argued in their academic works for a Germanisation and an ethnic new order in Eastern Europe. By doing so, they became to some extent intellectual trailblazers for the Holocaust.[130]

At the same time, the humanities could be components in a completely different kind of lifestyle or political identity. Research on the paperback revolution of the post-war era does more than simply draw attention to the importance of non-fiction books for knowledge circulation in the public sphere. Philipp Felsch has shown how, from the 1960s to the years around the fall of the Berlin Wall, the small publishing company Merve Verlag in West Berlin became an intellectual powerhouse for the boom in theory, both with respect to left-wing radicalism and postmodernism. Their paperbacks circulated in a city divided by the Cold War, and became not only a source of theoretical and political orientation but also material accessories for several generations of radical academics.[131]

The history of paperbacks shows that the division made here – between the humanities in the public sphere and in people's lives – can often be difficult to sustain on closer scrutiny. The circulation of humanistic knowledge in the public sphere could intervene in the lives of individuals and influence their identities, but the acquisition of knowledge by individuals could also have an impact on larger societal processes. However, in a broader knowledge-historical perspective this is not a paradox.

3.1.5 The History of Knowledge of Shareholding

The 1840s in England saw a rapid expansion of the country's railway network. This new infrastructure was financed not by the state but through limited companies acquiring capital from the general public. People who did not know each other – and who would never even meet one another – jointly invested money in high-risk companies. New legislation limited individual responsibility. It was impossible to lose more money than one had invested. If a company went bankrupt, the shareholders were not personally responsible for its debts.

This was referred to at the time as 'Railway Mania' or 'the Great Railway Craze'. The numbers here are instructive. In 1844, there were forty-eight railway companies in England. Two years later, there were 270. Statistics from the time also point to ownership being comparatively widespread. According to one investment manual, in the mid-nineteenth century 268,191 individuals owned railway shares. Most of these were financially well off, but

---
[129] Schöttler, *Geschichtsschreibung.*   [130] Aly, *Macht.*   [131] Felsch, *Der lange.*

there were also tens of thousands of people who had invested small sums. Among these were the authors and sisters Emily and Charlotte Brontë, who bought railway company shares for one pound each.

A prerequisite for the expansion of the railways in the 1840s was that information and knowledge circulated comparatively widely in society. This was done through newspapers and special periodicals. In England alone there were in 1845 twenty publications focusing on railway investments. But it was not just the readers of *The Daily Railway Share List* or *The Railway Courier* who could follow market developments. The ordinary daily press also published articles, price lists, and graphs over changes in the share prices of various railway companies. In addition, a large number of investment manuals were printed. Altogether, this information system created the preconditions for a geographically dispersed general public who shared financial knowledge and united for high-risk projects. A new type of more impersonal market began to take shape. Contemporaries spoke of a growing class of investors.[132]

Was this a societal breakthrough of knowledge? This is a matter of interpretation. If we compare it with the environmental turn from the years around 1970, we can see that in each case a qualitative change occurred when various kinds of knowledge went from being marginal phenomena to becoming forces to be reckoned with. But while the new shareholders were far more numerous in 1845 than in 1835, the overwhelming majority of people remained outside the market. Nevertheless, even these people were affected by the expansion of the railways, and many people who did not own shares read about and discussed them. The consequences of financial knowledge were great. The industrialisation and the emergence of modern society can hardly be understood without considering the expansion of the financial markets. Alongside the state, limited companies were the most important organisational form.

So how is it that limited companies and shareholding emerged in Europe? What is the longer history of this, and what role does knowledge play? From mediaeval marketplaces in cities such as Florence, Venice, and Bruges, a new financial system gradually emerged during the early modern age. It was a defining moment when in the sixteenth century state-sanctioned trading companies acquired status as legal persons, enabling merchants to practice joint ownership. However, it was not until the seventeenth century that these associations became permanent and the second-hand trade in owner's shares accelerated. Because of this, traders and others could spread their risk, but they could also engage in wild speculation. In 1720, the latter activity resulted in an infamous financial bubble in the English South Sea Company, in which the

---

[132] Preda, 'Rise'.

scientist Isaac Newton and others lost large parts of their fortunes. After this crash, English authorities adopted the so-called Bubble Act, which placed extensive restrictions on the formation of new limited companies well into the 1820s.[133]

Financial advice literature for private individuals can be traced back to the middle of the eighteenth century and the publication of navigator Thomas Mortimer's *Every Man His Own Broker; or, A Guide to Exchange-Alley* (1761). For decades, this work was unique, but around the turn of the century in 1800 the genre began to flourish. Since then books – of varying quality, reliability, and repute – have been published and have at times reached a large readership. Books such as George Clason's *The Richest Man in Babylon* (1926), Benjamin Graham's *The Intelligent Investor* (1949), and Burton Malkiel's *A Random Walk Down Wall Street* (1973) are all still in print.[134] Nevertheless, as Lendol Calder has pointed out, this type of literature still awaits its own historians. Only in recent years have a few research projects undertaken the mapping and analysis of these texts.[135] From a knowledge-historical perspective, this is thus an abundant, and still largely unprocessed, source material.

The importance of having knowledge about how financial markets function and of individuals taking an active part in them has increased over time, even though the development has been far from straightforward. Periods of intense societal circulation of financial knowledge, such as the 1920s, have been followed by periods of deep scepticism, such as the Great Depression of the 1930s. In the first decades of the post-war era, financial markets were strictly regulated, and not until the 1980s was there, in certain Western countries, a more significant expansion of shareholding and investing in mutual funds. In research, we speak of this in terms of a financialisation of the economy and society, or of a 'mass investment culture'.

It is characteristic of shareholding culture of the late twentieth and early twenty-first-centuries that financial knowledge has circulated on a completely new scale. This has been the case in both traditional mass media such as the press and TV and, from the late 1990s onwards, various digital fora and social media. The state has conducted large-scale information campaigns in connection with the privatisation of state-owned companies such as British Gas and British Telecom in the mid-1980s. Much hope has also been placed in educational efforts towards 'financial literacy'. But many commercial actors, not least banks and other financial institutions, have also played a central role in this. Additionally, special interest organisations and a large number of private individuals have taken an active interest in the circulation of knowledge.

---

[133] Broberg, *Konsten.*   [134] Chrostwaithe, 'Economic'.   [135] Calder, 'Saving'.

Today you can find so-called 'finfluencers' on Twitter/X, TikTok, and Facebook, as well as on blogs and net fora. All in all, this makes clear that financial knowledge is not something controlled by any single actor or institution. On the contrary, this is a field where many people attempt to make their voices heard and gain the trust of others. How these dynamics have developed over time is an important question for knowledge historians.[136]

One innovative way of studying this societal circulation is to investigate what preceded the intensification. After all, before one can put knowledge in motion by educating people, they must be made receptive. With respect to shares, it was necessary to eliminate deeply rooted negative ideas about the stock market. Before one could teach people how to best save money through shares, it was necessary for them to unlearn what they already knew.[137] In this area much remains to be done, but historians of knowledge are well equipped to accomplish this, not least those interested in how practical knowledge intervenes – and is concretely used – in people's everyday lives. In the following discussions, we will exemplify this with a Swedish shareholding contest that aimed to transform ordinary people into shareholders.

3.1.6 Knowledge about Shares in People's Lives

On 12 April 1979, the weekly *Veckans Affärer* (Weekly business) reported that schoolmistress Marianne Ejby had taken the lead in the ongoing Swedish shareholding championships. In one month, the value of her portfolio had risen by 17.7 per cent, while at the same time the Stockholm Stock Exchange as a whole had fallen by 6.9 per cent. This meant that she had won the first round. She was rewarded with a subscription to the magazine and five shares in an investment fund. This made her, for the first time in her life, a shareholder.

Marianne Ejby's knowledge of shares and business was, however, limited. She usually leafed past the business pages in the morning papers. The reason for her surprising victory in this round was that the shares into which she had placed the most money – Gotlandsbolaget – were the best-performing shares on the stock exchange. She had chosen to put money in the company because she had lived for six months in the town of Visby on the island of Gotland, and she liked the place very much. 'So one could really call my investment choice a stroke of good luck,' she said, laughing. But what was the contest Marianne Ejby had entered? And what makes it interesting for a historian of knowledge?

The Swedish shareholding championship (*Aktie-SM*) of 1979 was the first of its kind and was open to anyone who wanted to participate. The goal was to persuade people like Marianne Ejby to try their hand at investing on the stock

---

[136] Larsson Heidenblad, 'Financial'. [137] Husz, 'Making'.

exchange and realise how much fun it was and how educational and potentially profitable it could be to save money in shares. The hope was that investing in shares would become a larger part of the lives of more people. In the contest participants would place 25,000 virtual Swedish crowns (SEK) in a portfolio containing five different shares, investing at least 3,000 SEK in each share. The contest was launched in early March, and in November the first Swedish shareholding champion was announced. *Veckans Affärer* insisted that novices had as great a chance of winning the contest as did professionals. Special supplements to the magazine provided all the knowledge necessary for success. All that was needed was a bit of luck.

The Swedish shareholding championship attracted 50,000 participants and was considered a great success. Throughout the 1980s, further shareholding contests were arranged, along with variants such as national school championships and company championships. The ambition was, as it was phrased in an advertisement from 1981, to teach the participants 'how exciting and profitable it can be to invest money in shares'. Through the shareholding championships, this could be done 'without risking your own money'. Marianne Ejby's victory in the first round was exactly what the arrangers wanted. But after her initial success, she was replaced at the top by established stock exchange personalities.[138]

Not until 1984 did an amateur win the entire contest. This was twenty-seven-year-old secretary Lotta Nilsson, who had been persuaded by her colleagues to submit a coupon. 'It was pure luck that I won,' she explained to a tabloid. 'I put money in things I like: clothes, chocolate, cars.' This submission on the basis of pure guesswork, listing Hennes & Mauritz, Marabou, and Volvo, was enough for her to win the contest.

When an expert on the stock exchange learned about how she had justified her selections to the tabloid, he was stunned. He had himself won the shareholding championship once and had ended up in a top position several times. 'Can that really be true?' he said to the reporter. 'Well, all right then. Sometimes it's a disadvantage to be an expert. But I'm glad that she won. It's good publicity for the stock exchange.' Lotta Nilsson herself felt a bit embarrassed by all the attention. She was happy about the flowers, the victory banquet, and the upcoming trip to New York. But she really did not want to be portrayed as a stock exchange oracle by the evening papers. And she let experts invest her 10,000 SEK in prize money intended for buying shares.

In this way, Lotta Nilsson nevertheless became one of many new shareholders in Sweden in the 1980s. Contemporaries said that Sweden had

---

[138] Husz, 'Making'.

overtaken the United States as the country with the highest density of share-holders in the world. A large public opinion poll in 1983 indicated that one in every four Swedes, close to 1.8 million people, owned shares. In a little over a year, half a million new shareholders had been added. The reliability of the methods of measurement and the comparability of the national numbers are open to discussion, but the trend was clear. And it has, albeit with some bumps in the curve, continued up to our own time. In a few decades, shares had gone from being a phenomenon of a small social elite to something that concerns almost every adult Swede. Similar lines of development can be seen in many other Western countries, and during the twenty-first century we have been able to see how investing in shares has become increasingly popular in, for instance, India.[139]

Researchers have attempted to capture this major cultural change in personal economies with the phrase *the financialisation of everyday life*. By this, they meant that financial markets and practices have become an ever more important part of the lives of more and more people. But it also means that people adopt business administrative jargon and thinking in order to understand their personal lives, for instance by speaking of 'investing' in close relationships or discussing the 'yield' a certain educational course or working life experience can offer.[140] This is a development that would have been difficult to imagine at the end of the 1970s. At that time, neither shares nor financial markets were held in great esteem. Among politicians and citizens in Western Europe, there was widespread scepticism, and many people saw financial transactions as an unproductive and corrosive part of the societal economy. All around the world stock exchanges and banks were strictly regulated.

But at the same time, there were many people and organisations working for change. In the historiography of the market turn of the 1980s, right-wing politicians such as Margaret Thatcher in the United Kingdom and Ronald Reagan in the United States tend to be foregrounded, as well as neoliberal economists like Milton Friedman and the international network the Mont Pèlerin Society.[141] But did they actually create the change? Or did other forces pave the way? British historian Amy Edwards believes that those who want to understand the market turn of the 1980s must adopt a longer historical perspective. She points to factors such as the importance of the new popular journalism about personal finances that evolved during the 1960s and 1970s. In the so-called money pages, people learned about financial markets long before the privatisation of state-owned companies began.[142] If we look across the Atlantic

---

[139] Larsson Heidenblad, 'Marknadsleken'.   [140] Pellandini-Simányi, 'Financialization'.
[141] Mirowski, *Road*; Gerstle, *Rise*.   [142] Edwards, *Are We*.

to the American stock market culture, Janice Traflet shows that large campaigns were launched already in the 1940s and 1950s to transform common wage earners into shareholders. In this way, socialist tendencies would be suppressed and the future of free enterprise and the capitalist system would be secured.[143]

Questions regarding knowledge were central to all of this. In Sweden, a foundation for the promotion of shares, *Aktiefrämjandet* – established in 1976 – attempted to teach people about the social functions of the stock exchange. This was intended to correct what was felt to be a number of widespread misunderstandings. From the foundation's perspective, investing in shares was an excellent way for people to increase their knowledge about Swedish business, its prerequisites, and its merits. This was considered especially important at a time of economic crisis and high inflation.

To what extent Marianne Ejby, Lotta Nilsson, and the other participants in the national shareholding championship thought about these larger issues is difficult to know. The national shareholding championships were not perceived by their contemporaries as something political or controversial. It was a fun contest arranged by organisations connected to different segments of society. It is true that *Aktiefrämjandet* was bankrolled by business interests, but its chairman was a Social Democrat and the managing director was a Liberal. In addition, the contest was arranged by *Sparbankerna*, the Swedish savings banks, which were close to the labour movement. What this example shows is that an ambition to popularise investing in shares could bring together many different interests.

So what are the knowledge-historical consequences of the market turn? How have the ever increasing numbers of shareholders learned to buy and sell? Who do they listen to and trust? And how have the dynamics been affected by digitalisation, social media, user-friendly apps, and tax reforms? Questions such as these have begun to be explored in later years by historians of knowledge, but both the mapping and the analysis are still in their infancy. For those who want to study the knowledge of shares in people's lives there are good opportunities for contributing something genuinely new.

3.2 Knowledge in Circulation: Perspectives in Time and Space

With these examples – the breakthrough of the environmental movement, the history of the humanities, and the history of shares – we wanted to illustrate how the circulation of knowledge can be studied. We have in all three cases foregrounded both the movement of knowledge in society and the effect this has had on people's lives. In addition, we wished to illustrate how a knowledge-historical perspective can contribute to new scholarly questions taking centre

---

[143] Traflet, *A Nation*.

stage and new source materials, actors, and contexts becoming significant. The first example concerns knowledge in the natural sciences, but it is not the academic actors or the institutions of science that are essential. Using a knowledge-historical approach, we can instead show how a radical change in political and public consciousness came about with respect to environmental issues. The second example involves an expansion of the perception of humanists and their fields of activity, from the learned sphere to the broader public sphere. If the first example dealt with tipping points and breakthroughs of knowledge, we here emphasise continuities and the slow change of a humanistic culture of knowledge. The final case concerns a kind of everyday knowledge with comparatively weak links to established educational institutions such as schools and universities. This example shows how a knowledge-historical perspective can help us investigate socially important forms of knowledge that fall outside the framework of the histories of education and science.

Our three examples are rather specific, but we still want to believe that they contain more general knowledge-historical insights. At the same time, one can of course ask how universal our assumptions and approaches are. We have mainly dealt with the modern period, with a certain emphasis on the post-war era, and geographically we have remained mainly in Western Europe and North America. Are our analytic concepts and frameworks useful also with respect to other times and places?

Kajsa Weber, an expert on the history of early modern books and knowledge, has challenged us on these points. She argues that the understanding of society that forms the basis of our concept of the *societal circulation of knowledge* is only applicable to modern history and not valid in older contexts. Weber maintains that in early modern society a certain type of knowledge was reserved mainly for small societal groups, for example learned or ecclesiastical associations. In that society there was a strong sense of the legitimacy of hierarchical orders, and there was no egalitarian ideal like the one found in democratic mass societies. This meant that in the pre-modern period the circulation of at least certain kinds of knowledge by definition was an elite phenomenon, and that it is difficult to argue for a broader societal breakthrough.[144] It is possible that it was not before the emergence of a civic public sphere in the eighteenth and nineteenth centuries, with a press corps and a new kind of book market, that preconditions were created for the kind of societal circulation of knowledge exemplified above.

Other researchers could challenge us on other points. For instance, Federico Marcon, a historian specialising in early modern Japan, has emphasised the risk of uncritically using knowledge-historical perspectives developed in a Western

---

[144] Weber, 'Circulation'.

research context for conditions in, say, East Asia.[145] Maria Bach, who has investigated Indian economists of the nineteenth century, has in a similar way contributed to problematising Western starting points in the study of the history of knowledge.[146] Global historian Lisa Hellman has also sounded a note of caution. She has pointed out the necessity of analysing the global dynamics of power in the production and circulation of knowledge, especially the importance of considering 'coerced actors' and their limited room to manoeuvre.[147]

The question then becomes how universal our analytical concepts – such as *knowledge arena*, *knowledge actor*, and *circulation of knowledge* – actually are. These are interesting reflections worth considering, and they deserve serious discussion and empirical examination. More generally, these points of view indicate the importance of historians of knowledge not limiting themselves to one particular period, geographical area, or segment of society, but instead remaining open to impetuses and insights from researchers with specialities other than their own. We hope therefore that the international knowledge-historical community will also in future embrace researchers with diverse specialities and backgrounds.

4 The Future of the History of Knowledge

In September 1936, András István Gróf was born in a middle-class Jewish family in Budapest. He lived there for his first twenty years, some of them under a false identity. During the Nazi occupation of Hungary in 1944, his father was deported to a labour camp. The family was not reunited until after the war. The Hungarian revolution followed in 1956, an uprising against the country's Communist dictatorship. This was struck down by Soviet Union military intervention and in November armed resistance ceased. By this time, however, András István Gróf had already fled across the border to Austria. In 1957, he moved from there to the United States. He could barely speak English and had no economic assets, but was determined to create a new life. In order to fit into his new country, he changed his name to Andrew Grove.

In the United States, he began to study chemistry, first in New York and later in California. In 1963, he published his thesis at Berkeley and was then hired by Fairchild Semiconductor. During his years there, he wrote a textbook in chemistry and became acquainted with many other ambitious people. In 1968, two of these started the company Intel, and immediately hired Andrew Grove. During the next five decades he was, in various ways, deeply involved in Silicon Valley and the emergence of digital society. At his death in 2016, he was one of the most respected corporate managers in the United States.

---

[145] Marcon, 'Critical'.   [146] Bach, 'Marginalised'.   [147] Hellman, 'Grappling'.

Andrew Grove's dramatic life journey sheds light on central processes in the history of knowledge of the twentieth century. It is a history replete with violent political conflict, repression, and tension between East and West. It is a history of separation and migration. But it is also a history of higher education, rapid technological development, and innovative companies. Through actors like Andrew Grove we can see how interwoven these historical processes are. It is not surprising that many researchers today find the combination of the history of knowledge and the history of migration particularly fruitful.[148]

Other historians of knowledge are interested in digitalisation as such, and the emergence of a new type of society: the knowledge society. This concept was coined at the end of the 1960s by American social scientists and intellectuals such as Daniel Bell and Peter Drucker. They maintained that the Western world had entered a new post-industrial state. Here it was no longer raw materials, factories, and labour that created wealth. Instead, people's knowledge was the most important thing. It was felt that the collected body of knowledge was in a state of exponential growth. When thinkers looked towards the future, they predicted that knowledge – and advanced forms of knowledge work – would only become more important. These ideas were adopted in the 1970s by sociologists and economists, as well as by politicians and journalists. Gradually, the knowledge society became self-defining. Was the tipping point perhaps the economic structural crisis of the late 1970s, when the West began to deindustrialise in earnest and the service sector began to expand? Or was it the introduction of personal computers into the home that created the shift? What about the Internet and stable broadband connections?

To a large extent, the history of the knowledge society still remains to be written. The chronology is uncertain, and the periodisation is tentative. In addition, there are still no substantial studies of how the concept itself emerged and was understood over time, along with closely related concepts such as the information society and the communication society. Nor do we know more than very generally how the emergence of the knowledge society is related to other major social transformations – such as globalisation, Europeanisation, financialisaton, and medialisation. What would happen if we were to look more closely at these developments? Would we see new lines and tipping points that the traditional economic, political, and social historiography overlooks?

We believe this to be the case. And here we can return to Andrew Grove. What is his place in the historiography of the post-war era? Had you heard of him and *Only the Paranoid Survive* before reading this book? Was Intel perhaps only a logo on your computer? An invisible part of the digital infrastructure on

---

[148] Lässig and Steinberg, 'Knowledge'; Burke, 'Exiles'; Zloch, *Das Wissen*.

which we today are completely dependent? This would not surprise us. A few years ago his name was unknown to us, too. And this is of course always the case. Most things – in our present and in the past – we as individuals know nothing about. But this should not prevent us from seeking to clarify how things once were, and attempting to provide answers to why the world looks the way it does now. Exploring this is the task of historians, and it is never complete.

There are also other reasons why one should study the history of knowledge. When we began our work exploring and developing this new field in the middle of the 2010s, we justified our research specialisation by saying it could contribute to illuminating the contemporary knowledge society. Historising the knowledge society seemed to be an important task at a time when so many political and economic hopes were tied to school, the university, and other knowledge-bearing and knowledge-generating institutions. We still believe this to be true.[149]

Since then, however, an epistemic change of atmosphere has occurred in society. Populism's political success and the return of authoritarianism in our part of the world has introduced new discourses into public debate. 'Fake news' and 'alternative facts' are concepts that have been used by powerful political leaders, both to deny election results and sow doubt about global warming. During the pandemic, conspiracy theories acquired many followers, not least when they were channelled via social media, while at the same time traditional scientific experts appeared in public and asserted their own authority. Human suffering aside, Russia's full-scale war of aggression against Ukraine is also an information and propaganda war. Consequently, the drama of recent years has, in many ways, disturbed our knowledge systems.

How the coming years will turn out is shrouded in mystery, but with the aid of historical insight we can hopefully better navigate through revolutionary times. The technical and media changes will certainly continue to disrupt the conditions for the production and circulation of knowledge. At the time of writing, a discussion about artificial intelligence is in full swing, and it is highly likely that computer programs and robots that emulate human intelligence and cognitive functions in future will have an impact on knowledge in society and in people's lives. In the not-too-distant future, our political, cultural, and economic lives will be dominated by the first generation to be born digital. At the same time there will be, for many decades to come, many people who grew up in a distinctly analogue world where newspapers on paper, printed books, and broadcast media formed the basis of the media landscape. As so often is the case

---

[149] Östling, 'Vad är'.

in history, different knowledge systems and forms of knowledge will coexist and overlap.

It is our conviction that the history of knowledge is a field of research that has great potential for the future. What we especially hope is that it will help historians write more comprehensive social histories with a strong relevance for our own time and self-understanding. We have great faith in the paths that we have primarily argued for – studying knowledge as a greater social phenomenon as well as investigating how knowledge intervenes in people's lives. But exactly what the field will consist of, or how it will develop, remains to be seen. History is a collective knowledge project, and it is neither possible nor desirable to control it in detail. We look forward to being challenged, surprised, and inspired.

Further Reading

In this Element, we have described how the history of knowledge has developed as a new scholarly field in the twenty-first century, especially in the most recent decade. In order to allow for a better orientation among the publications that have contributed to the formation of the field and to provide for more detailed perusal of selected subjects, theories, and questions, we have here collected a number of recommendations for further reading, with preference given to works available in English.

The history of knowledge as a field is discussed in Martin Mulsow and Lorraine Daston, 'History of Knowledge', in Marek Tamm and Peter Burke (eds.), *Debating New Approaches to History*. London: Bloomsbury Academic, 2019; Suzanne Marchand, 'How Much Knowledge Is Worth Knowing? An American Intellectual Historian's Thoughts on the *Geschichte des Wissens*', *Berichte zur Wissenschaftsgeschichte* 42:2–3 (2019); Sven Dupré and Geert Somson, 'What Is the History of Knowledge?', *Journal for the History of Knowledge* 1:1 (2020); Helge Jordheim and David Gary Shaw, 'Opening Doors: A Turn to Knowledge', *History and Theory* 59:4 (2020); and Charlotte A. Lerg, Johan Östling, and Jana Weiss, 'Introducing the Yearbook *History of Intellectual Culture*', in Charlotte A. Lerg, Johan Östling, and Jana Weiss (eds.), *History of Intellectual Culture: International Yearbook of Knowledge and Society*, vol. 1. Berlin: De Gruyter, 2022.

Historiographic overviews of the history of knowledge include Johan Östling et al., 'The History of Knowledge and the Circulation of Knowledge: An Introduction', in Johan Östling et al. (eds.), *Circulation of Knowledge: Explorations in the History of Knowledge*. Lund: Nordic Academic Press, 2018; Marian Füssel, 'Wissensgeschichten der Frühen

Neuzeit: Begriffe–Themen–Probleme', in Marian Füssel (ed.), *Wissensgeschichte*. Stuttgart: Franz Steiner Verlag, 2019; Johan Östling, David Larsson Heidenblad, and Anna Nilsson Hammar, 'Developing the History of Knowledge', in Johan Östling, David Larsson Heidenblad, and Anna Nilsson Hammar (eds.), *Forms of Knowledge: Developing the History of Knowledge*. Lund: Nordic Academic Press, 2020; Johan Östling, 'Circulation, Arenas, and the Quest for Public Knowledge: Historiographical Currents and Analytical Frameworks', *History and Theory* 59:4 (2020a); and Joel Barnes and Tamson Pietsch, 'The History of Knowledge and the History of Education', *History of Education Review* 33:1 (2022).

In several programmatic articles, historians of various persuasions have defined the history of knowledge and provided their ideas of what should be included. See, for example, Philipp Sarasin, 'Was ist Wissensgeschichte?', *Internationales Archiv für Sozialgeschichte in der deutschen Literatur* 36:1 (2011); Simone Lässig, 'The History of Knowledge and the Expansion of the Historical Research Agenda', *Bulletin of the German Historical Institute* 59 (2016); Lorraine Daston, 'The History of Science and the History of Knowledge', *KNOW: A Journal on the Formation of Knowledge* 1:1 (2017); Shadi Bartsch et al., 'Editors' Introduction', *KNOW: A Journal on the Formation of Knowledge* 1:1 (2017); Johan Östling and David Larsson Heidenblad, 'Fulfilling the Promise of the History of Knowledge: Key Approaches for the 2020s', *Journal for the History of Knowledge* 1:1 (2020); and Philipp Sarasin, 'More Than Just Another Speciality: On the Prospects for the History of Knowledge', *Journal for the History of Knowledge* 1:1 (2020). One of the most rewarding analytic concepts in the field is that of the circulation of knowledge. Here historians of knowledge have built upon discussions in the history of science, not least with a starting point in James A. Secord, 'Knowledge in Transit', *Isis* 95:4 (2004); and Kapil Raj, *Relocating Modern Science: Circulation and the Construction of Knowledge in South Asia and Europe, 1650–1900*. Basingstoke: Palgrave Macmillan, 2007.

In a number of books the authors have adopted a more comprehensive approach to the field and have contributed to the introduction of knowledge-historical perspectives, usually by combining general lines of reasoning with empirical exemplification. Peter Burke has published half a dozen books on the history of knowledge, including overviews such as *A Social History of Knowledge: From Gutenberg to Diderot*. Cambridge: Polity Press, 2000; and *A Social History of Knowledge: From the Encyclopédie to Wikipedia*. Cambridge: Polity Press, 2012; an introductory work such as *What Is the History of Knowledge?* Cambridge: Polity Press, 2016; and thematic works like *Ignorance: A Global History*. New Haven: Yale University Press, 2023.

Christian Jacob is responsible for the two-volume *Lieux de savoir*. Paris: Michel, 2007–2011 and *Des mondes lettrés aux lieux de savoir*. Paris: Les Belles Lettres, 2018. Marian Füssel has published the introductory book *Wissen: Konzepte – Praktiken – Prozesse*. Frankfurt am Main: Campus Verlag, 2021 as well as an anthology of key texts, *Wissensgeschichte*. Stuttgart: Franz Steiner Verlag, 2019. We have ourselves, together with our colleagues, produced a history of knowledge trilogy: *Circulation of Knowledge: Explorations in the History of Knowledge*. Lund: Nordic Academic Press, 2018; *Forms of Knowledge: Developing the History of Knowledge*. Lund: Nordic Academic Press, 2020; and *Knowledge Actors: Revisiting Agency in the History of Knowledge*. Lund: Nordic Academic Press, 2023.

Periodical publications have also been significant for the establishment of the history of knowledge field. *Nach Feierabend* (Diaphanes), a yearbook published from 2005 to 2020 by Zentrum Geschichte des Wissens in Zürich, was among the pioneers; its final issue includes retrospective reflections on its publication by, among others, Sandra Bärnreuther, Maria Böhmer, and Sophie Witt, 'Editorial: Feierabend? (Rück-)Blicke auf "Wissen"', *Nach Feierabend*. Zürich: Diaphanes, 2020. *KNOW: A Journal on the Formation of Knowledge* (University of Chicago Press), the first issue of which was published in 2017, has Shadi Bartsch-Zimmer as its editor-in-chief and is an official publication of the Stevanovich Institute on the Formation of Knowledge at the University of Chicago, while the *Journal for the History of Knowledge* (Ubiquity Press; editors-in chief: Sven Dupré and Geert Somsen), which published its first issue in 2020, is affiliated with Gewina, the Belgian-Dutch Society for History of Science and Universities. The first volume of a yearbook with a history of knowledge focus, *History of Intellectual Culture: International Yearbook of Knowledge and Society* (De Gruyter) was published in 2022, with Charlotte A. Lerg, Johan Östling, and Jana Weiß as editors. In addition, several journals have devoted special issues or thematic sections to the history of knowledge, including *Geschichte und Gesellschaft*, *History and Theory*, *Kulturstudier*, *Slagmark*, *History of Humanities*, *History of Education Review*, and *Nordic Journal of Educational History*.

Several academic book series have a history of knowledge focus: Knowledge Societies in History, Routledge (editors Sven Dupré and Wijnand Mijnhardt); Global Epistemics, Rowman & Littlefield International (editor Inanna Hamati-Ataya); Studies in the History of Knowledge, Amsterdam University Press (editors Klaas van Berkel, Jeroen van Dongen, and Herman Paul); and History of Science & Knowledge, Princeton University Press (editor Eric Crahan). Among the books that have been published in these series can be mentioned, for example, Johan Östling, Niklas Olsen, and David

Larsson Heidenblad (eds.), *Histories of Knowledge in Postwar Scandinavia: Actors, Arenas, and Aspirations*. Abingdon: Routledge, 2020; Anders Ekström and Hampus Östh Gustafsson (eds.), *The Humanities and the Modern Politics of Knowledge: The Impact and Organization of the Humanities in Sweden, 1850–2020*. Amsterdam: Amsterdam University Press, 2022; Renate Dürr (ed.), *Threatened Knowledge: Practices of Knowing and Ignoring from the Middle Ages to the Twentieth Century*. Abingdon, Routledge, 2022; and Lorraine Daston, *Rules: A Short History of What We Live By*. Princeton: Princeton University Press, 2022.

In addition to these works, a number of monographs based on a history of knowledge framework have been published in the 2020s. Here, we find large-scale presentations such as Jürgen Renn, *The Evolution of Knowledge: Rethinking Science for the Anthropocene*. Princeton: Princeton University Press, 2020; and Rens Bod, *World of Patterns: A Global History of Knowledge*. Baltimore: Johns Hopkins University Press, 2022, but also more specialised studies like Kijan Espahangizi, *Der Migration-Integration-Komplex: Wissenschaft und Politik in einem (Nicht-)Einwanderungsland, 1960–2010*. Göttingen: Konstanz University Press, 2022; Joshua Ehrlich, *The East India Company and the Politics of Knowledge*. Cambridge: Cambridge University Press, 2023; and Stephanie Zloch, *Das Wissen der Einwanderungsgesellschaft: Migration und Bildung in Deutschland 1945–2000*. Göttingen: Wallstein Verlag, 2023. A number of doctoral dissertations have also been presented, including, to cite a few Nordic examples, Susann Holmberg (University of Oslo, 2020), Sine Halkjelsvik Bjordal (University of Oslo, 2021), Andreas Granberg (Åbo Akademi University, 2022), and Mikko Myllyntausta (University of Turku, 2022). Finally, our own monographs can be mentioned: Johan Östling, *Humboldt and the Modern German University: An Intellectual History*. Lund: Lund University Press, 2018; David Larsson Heidenblad, *The Environmental Turn in Postwar Sweden: A New History of Knowledge*. Lund: Lund University Press, 2021; and Johan Östling, Anton Jansson, and Ragni Svensson Stringberg, *Humanister i offentligheten: Kunskapens aktörer och arenor under efterkrigstiden*. Gothenburg and Stockholm: Makadam, 2022.

Bibliography

'About the Journal', *Journal for the History of Knowledge*, accessed 20 May 2020. https://journalhistoryknowledge.org/about/.

Ahlstedt Åberg, Måns, 'Amateur Eugenics: The "Great-Mother in Dalecarlia" Genealogy Project and the Collaboration between the Swedish Institute for Race Biology and the General Public, 1930–1935', in Charlotte A. Lerg, Johan Östling, and Jana Weiß (eds.), *History of Intellectual Culture: International Yearbook of Knowledge and Society*, Vol. 1 (2022). Berlin: De Gruyter, 124–46. https://doi:10.1515/9783110748819-007.

Aly, Götz, *Macht – Geist – Wahn: Kontinuitäten deutschen Denkens*. Berlin: Argon, 1997.

Bach, Maria, 'Marginalised Actors of Knowledge', in Johan Östling, David Larsson Heidenblad, and Anna Nilsson Hammar (eds.), *Knowledge Actors: Revisiting Agency in the History of Knowledge*. Lund: Nordic Academic Press, 2023, 121–38.

Barnes, Joel, 'Knowledge in the Air: Circulation, Actors and Arenas of Knowledge', in Johan Östling, David Larsson Heidenblad, and Anna Nilsson Hammar (eds.), *Knowledge Actors: Revisiting Agency in the History of Knowledge*. Lund: Nordic Academic Press, 2023, 201–16.

Barnes, Joel, and Tamson Pietsch, 'The History of Knowledge and the History of Education', *History of Education Review* 51:2 (2022), 109–22. http://doi:10.1108/HER-06-2022-0020.

Barth, Fredrik, 'An Anthropology of Knowledge', *Current Anthropology* 43:1 (2002). 1–18. https://doi.org/10.1086/324131.

Bartsch, Shadi, Clifford Ando, Robert J. Richards, and Haun Saussy, 'Editors' Introduction', *KNOW: A Journal on the Formation of Knowledge* 1:1 (2017), 201–09. https://doi.org/10.1086/692273.

Bayly, Christopher, *The Birth of the Modern World, 1780–1914: Global Connections and Comparisons*. Oxford: Blackwell, 2004.

Berg, Annika, Christina Florin, and Per Wisselgren (eds.), *Par i vetenskap och politik: Intellektuella äktenskap i moderniteten*. Umeå: Borea, 2011.

Bergwik Staffan, and Linn Holmberg, 'Standing on Whose Shoulders? A Critical Comment on the History of Knowledge', in Johan Östling, David Larsson Heidenblad, and Anna Nilsson Hammar, (eds.), *Forms of Knowledge*. Lund: Nordic Academic Press, 2020. 283–99.

Blair, Ann, *Too Much to Know: Managing Scholarly Information before the Modern Age*. New Haven: Yale University Press, 2010.

Bod, Rens, Julia Kursell, Jaap Maat, and Thijs Weststeijn, 'A New Field: History of Humanities', *History of Humanities* 1:1 (2016), 1–8. https://doi.org/10.1086/685056.

Bod, Rens, *World of Patterns: A Global History of Knowledge.* Baltimore: Johns Hopkins University Press, 2022.

Bodensten, Erik, 'A Societal History of Potato Knowledge in Sweden c. 1650–1800', *Scandinavian Journal of History* 46:1 (2021), 42–62. http://doi:10.1080/03468755.2020.1752301.

Bonnell, Victoria, and Lynn Hunt, *Beyond the Cultural Turn: New Directions in the Study of Society and Culture.* Berkeley: University of California Press, 1999.

Bourdieu, Pierre, *Homo Academicus.* Paris: Éd. de Minuit, 1984.

Boyer, Paul S., *By the Bomb's Early Light: American Thought and Culture at the Dawn of the Atomic Age.* Chapel Hill: University of North Carolina Press, 1994 (1985).

Broberg, Oskar, *Konsten att skapa pengar: Aktiebolagens genombrott och finansiell modernisering kring sekelskiftet 1900.* Gothenburg: University of Gothenburg, 2006.

Burke, Peter, *A Social History of Knowledge: From Gutenberg to Diderot.* Cambridge: Polity Press, 2000.

Burke, Peter, *A Social History of Knowledge: From the Encyclopédie to Wikipedia.* Cambridge: Polity Press, 2012.

Burke, Peter, *Exiles and Expatriates in the History of Knowledge, 1500–2000.* Waltham: Brandeis University Press, 2017.

Burke, Peter, *Ignorance: A Global History.* New Haven: Yale University Press, 2023.

Burke, Peter, *The Polymath: A Cultural History from Leonardo da Vinci to Susan Sontag.* New Haven: Yale University Press, 2020.

Burke, Peter, *What Is the History of Knowledge?* Cambridge: Polity Press, 2016.

Calder, Lendol, 'Saving and Spending', in Frank Trentmann (ed.), *The Oxford Handbook of the History of Consumption.* Oxford: Oxford University Press, 2012, 348–75.

Coodley, Gregg, and David Sarasohn, *The Green Years, 1964–1976: When Democrats and Republicans United to Repair the Earth.* Lawrence: University Press of Kansas, 2021.

Cross, Gary, 'The "Silent Springs" of Rachel Carson: Mass Media and the Origins of Modern Environmentalism', *Public Understanding of Science* 10:4 (2001), 403–20. https://doi.org/10.3109/a036878

Crosthwaite, Paul, Peter Knight, and Nicky Marsh, 'The Economic Humanities and the History of Financial Advice', *American Literary History* 31:4 (2019), 661–86. http://doi:10.1093/alh/ajz031.

Daston, Lorraine, 'The History of Science and the History of Knowledge', *KNOW: A Journal on the Formation of Knowledge* 1:1 (2017), 132–54. https://doi.org/10.1086/691678.

Daston, Lorraine, and H. Otto Sibum, 'Introduction: Scientific Personae and Their Histories', *Science in Context* 16:1–2 (2003), 1–8. http://doi:10.1017/S026988970300067X.

Döring, Jörg, Sonja Lewandowski, and David Oels (eds.), *Rowohlts deutsche Enzyklopädie: Wissenschaft im Taschenbuch 1955–68*. Hannover: Wehrhahn Verlag, 2017.

Dupré, Sven, and Christine Göttler (eds.), *Knowledge and Discernment in the Early Modern Arts*. London: Routledge, 2017.

Echterhölter, Anna, 'Shells and Order: Questionnaires on Indigenous Law in German New Guinea', *Journal for the History of Knowledge* 1:1 (2020), 1–19. http://doi:10.5334/jhk.45.

Edelstein, Dan, Paula Findlen, Giovanna Ceserani, Caroline Winterer, and Nicole Coleman, 'Historical Research in a Digital Age: Reflections from the Mapping the Republic of Letters Project', *The American Historical Review* 122:2 (2017), 400–24. https://doi.org/10.1093/ahr/122.2.400.

Edwards, Amy, *Are We Rich Yet? The Rise of Mass Investment Culture in Contemporary Britain*. Oakland: University of California Press, 2022.

Ehrlich, Joshua, *The East India Company and the Politics of Knowledge*. Cambridge: Cambridge University Press, 2023.

Eisenstein, Elizabeth, *The Printing Revolution in Early Modern Europe*. Cambridge: Cambridge University Press, 2005.

Engblom, Lars-Åke, *Radio- och TV-folket: Rekryteringen av programmedarbetare till radion och televisionen i Sverige 1925–1995*. Stockholm: Rabén Prisma, 1998.

Felsch, Philipp, *Der lange Sommer der Theorie: Geschichte einer Revolte 1960–1990*. München: C.H. Beck, 2015.

Felten, Sebastian, and Christine von Oertzen, 'Bureaucracy as Knowledge', *Journal for the History of Knowledge* 1:1 (2020), 1–16. http://doi:10.5334/jhk.45.

Findlen, Paula (ed.), *Empires of Knowledge: Scientific Networks in the Early Modern World*. New York: Routledge, 2018.

Fischer-Tiné, Harald, *Pidgin-Knowledge: Wissen und Kolonialismus*. Zürich: Diaphanes, 2013.

Füssel, Marian, *Wissensgeschichte*. Stuttgart: Franz Steiner Verlag, 2019.

Füssel, Marian, *Wissen: Konzepte – Praktiken – Prozesse*. Frankfurt am Main: Campus Verlag, 2021.

Geertz, Clifford, *The Interpretation of Cultures: Selected Essays*. New York: Basic Books, 2017.

Gerstle, Gary, *The Rise and Fall of the Neoliberal Order*. Oxford: Oxford University Press, 2022.

Glückler, Johannes, Roy Suddaby, and Regina Lenz (eds.), *Knowledge and Institutions*. Cham: Springer, 2018.

Grove, Andrew S., *Only the Paranoid Survive: How to Exploit the Crisis Points That Challenge Every Company and Career*. New York: Currency Doubleday, 1996.

Guha, Ramachandra, *Environmentalism: A Global History*. New York: Longman, 2000.

Hall, Edith, and Henry Stead, *A People's History of Classics: Class and Greco-Roman Antiquity in Britain and Ireland, 1689 to 1939*. London: Routledge, 2020.

Hammar, Isak, and Hampus Östh Gustafsson, 'Unity Lost: Negotiating the Ancient Roots of Pedagogy in Sweden, 1865–1971', *History of Education Review* 51:2 (2022), 137–53. https://doi:10.1108/HER-04-2021-0007.

Hammar, Isak, and Johan Östling (eds.), 'Forum: The Circulation of Knowledge and the History of Humanities. Introduction', *History of Humanities* 6:2 (2021), 595–602. https://doi.org/10.1086/715941.

Hellman, Lisa, 'Grappling with Actors of Knowledge: A View from Global History', in Johan Östling, David Larsson Heidenblad, and Anna Nilsson Hammar (eds.), *Knowledge Actors: Revisiting Agency in the History of Knowledge*. Lund: Nordic Academic Press, 2023.

Hemmungs Wirtén, Eva, *Making Marie Curie: Intellectual Property and Celebrity Culture in an Age of Information*. Chicago: University of Chicago Press, 2015.

Hoeres, Peter, *Zeitung für Deutschland: Die Geschichte der FAZ*. München: Benevento, 2019.

Hunt, Lynn (ed.), *The New Cultural History*. Berkeley: University of California Press, 1989.

Husz, Orsi, and David Larsson Heidenblad, 'The Making of Everyman's Capitalism in Sweden: Micro-Infrastructures, Unlearning, and Moral Boundary Work', *Enterprise & Society* 24:2 (2023), 1–30. https://doi:10.1017/eso.2021.41.

Jansson, Anton, 'Things Are Different Elsewhere: An Intellectual History of Intellectual History in Sweden', *Global Intellectual History* 6:1 (2021), 83–94. https://doi:10.1080/23801883.2019.1657634.

Jülich, Solveig, Patrik Lundell, and Pelle Snickars, *Mediernas kulturhistoria*. Stockholm: Mediehistoriskt arkiv, 2008.

Kärnfelt, Johan, Karl Grandin, and Solveig Jülich (eds.), *Knowledge in Motion: The Royal Swedish Academy of Sciences and the Making of Modern Society*. Gothenburg: Makadam, 2018.

Krämer, Fabian, 'Shifting Demarcations: An Introduction', *History of Humanities* 3:1 (2018), 5–14. https://doi.org/10.1086/696298.

Kroll, Gary, 'The "Silent Springs" of Rachel Carson: Mass Media and the Origins of Modern Environmentalism', *Public Understanding of Science* 10:4 (2001), 403–20. http://doi:10.1088/0963-6625/10/4/304.

Küçük, Harun, 'The Bureaucratic Sense of the Forthcoming in Seventeenth-Century Istanbul', *Journal for the History of Knowledge* 1:1 (2020), 1–16. http://doi:10.5334/jhk.22.

Larsen, Lillian, and Samuel Rubenson (eds.), *Monastic Education in Late Antiquity: The Transformation of Classical Paideia*. Cambridge: Cambridge University Press, 2018.

Larsson Heidenblad, David, 'Environmental History in the 1960s? An Unsuccessful Research Application and the Circulation of Environmental Knowledge', *History of Humanities* 6:2 (2021), 635–47. https://doi.org/10.1086/715944.

Larsson Heidenblad, David, *The Environmental Turn in Postwar Sweden: A New History of Knowledge*. Lund: Lund University Press, 2021.

Larsson Heidenblad, David, *Vårt eget fel: Moralisk kausalitet som tankefigur från 00-talets klimatlarm till förmoderna syndastraffsföreställningar*. Höör: Agering, 2012.

Larsson Heidenblad, David, and Johan Östling, 'Efterord: Nordisk kunskapshistoria inför 2020-talet', *Kulturstudier* 10:2 (2019), 198–202. https://doi.org/10.7146/ks.v10i2.118023.

Lässig, Simone, 'The History of Knowledge and the Expansion of the Historical Research Agenda', *Bulletin of the German Historical Institute* 59 (2016), 29–58.

Leong, Elaine, *Recipes and Everyday Knowledge: Medicine, Science, and the Household in Early Modern England*. Chicago: University of Chicago Press, 2018.

Lightman, Bernard V., Gordon McOuat, and Larry Stewart (eds.), *The Circulation of Knowledge between Britain, India, and China: The Early-Modern World to the Twentieth Century*. Leiden: Brill, 2013.

Lowe, Roy, and Yoshihito Yasuhara, *The Origins of Higher Learning: Knowledge Networks and the Early Development of Universities*. London: Routledge, 2017.

Lundberg, Björn, 'Exploring the History of Knowledge and Education: An Introduction', *Nordic Journal of Educational History* 9:2 (2022), 1–11. https://doi:10.36368/njedh.v9i2.350.

Lundberg, Björn, 'Youth Activism and Global Awareness: The Emergence of the *Operation Dagsverke* Campaign in 1960s Sweden', *Contemporary European History*, First View (2022), 1–15. https://doi:10.1017/S0960777322000595.

Lundgren, Lars. J., *Acid Rain on the Agenda: A Picture of a Chain of Events in Sweden, 1966–1968*. Lund: Lund University Press, 1998.

Marchand, Suzanne, 'Weighing Context and Practices: Theodor Mommsen and the Many Dimensions of Nineteenth-Century Humanistic Knowledge', *History and Theory* 59:4 (2020), 144–67. https://doi:10.1111/hith.12187.

Marcon, Federico, 'The Critical Promises of the History of Knowledge: Perspectives from East Asian Studies', *History and Theory* 59:4 (2020), 19–47. https://doi:10.1111/hith.12180.

Mercer, Ben, 'The Paperback Revolution: Mass-Circulation Books and the Cultural Origins of 1968 in Western Europe', *Journal of the History of Ideas* 72:4 (2011), 613–36. https://doi:10.1353/jhi.2011.0032.

Mirowski, Philipp, and Diether Plehwe (eds.), *The Road from Mont Pèlerin: The Making of the Neoliberal Thought Collective*. Cambridge, MA: Harvard University Press, 2009.

Mulsow, Martin, and Lorraine Daston, 'History of Knowledge', in Marek Tamm, and Peter Burke (eds.), *Debating New Approaches to History*. London: Bloomsbury Academic, 2019. 159–88.

Nilsson Hammar, Anna, 'Theoria, Praxis and Poiesis: Theoretical Considerations on the Circulation of Knowledge in Everyday Life', in Johan Östling, Erling Sandmo, David Larsson Heidenblad, Anna Nilsson Hammar, and Kari H. Nordberg (eds.), *Circulation of Knowledge: Explorations in the History of Knowledge*. Lund: Nordic Academic Press, 2018, 107–24.

Nilsson Hammar, Anna, and Svante Norrhem, 'The Capacity to Act: On Phronetic Knowledge among the Less Privileged in Seventeenth-Century Sweden', in Johan Östling, David Larsson Heidenblad, and Anna Nilsson Hammar (eds.), *Knowledge Actors: Revisiting Agency in the History of Knowledge*. Lund: Nordic Academic Press, 2023, 139–57.

O'Mara, Margaret, *The Code: Silicon Valley and the Remaking of America*. New York: Penguin Press, 2019.

Östling, Johan, 'Circulation, Arenas, and the Quest for Public Knowledge: Historiographical Currents and Analytical Frameworks', *History and Theory* 59:4 (2020), 111–26. https://doi:10.1111/hith.12184.

Östling, Johan, 'Kunskap', in Jonas Hansson, and Kristiina Savin (eds.), *Svenska begreppshistorier: Från antropocen till åsiktskorridor.* Stockholm: Fri tanke, 2022, 309–16.

Östling, Johan, 'Vad är kunskapshistoria?', *Historisk tidskrift* 135:1 (2015), 109–19.

Östling, Johan, Anton Jansson, and Ragni Svensson Stringberg, *Humanister i offentligheten: Kunskapens aktörer och arenor under efterkrigstiden.* Gothenburg and Stockholm: Makadam, 2022.

Östling, Johan, Anton Jansson, and Ragni Svensson, 'Public Arenas of the Humanities: The Circulation of Knowledge in the Postwar Period', in Anders Ekström, and Hampus Östh Gustafsson (eds.), *The Humanities and the Modern Politics of Knowledge: The Impact and Organization of the Humanities in Sweden 1800–2020.* Amsterdam: Amsterdam University Press, 2022, 155–78. https://doi:10.2307/j.ctv2svjznh.9.

Östling, Johan, David Larsson Heidenblad, and Anna Nilsson Hammar, 'Developing the History of Knowledge', in Johan Östling, David Larsson Heidenblad, and Anna Nilsson Hammar (eds.), *Forms of Knowledge: Developing the History of Knowledge.* Lund: Nordic Academic Press, 2020, 9–26.

Östling, Johan, and David Larsson Heidenblad, 'Fulfilling the Promise of the History of Knowledge: Key Approaches for the 2020s', *Journal for the History of Knowledge* 1:1 (2020), 1–6. https://doi:10.5334/jhk.24.

Östling, Johan, David Larsson Heidenblad, and Anna Nilsson Hammar (eds.), *Knowledge Actors: Revisiting Agency in the History of Knowledge.* Lund: Nordic Academic Press, 2023.

Östling, Johan, Erling Sandmo, David Larsson Heidenblad, Anna Nilsson Hammar, and Kari H. Nordberg (eds.), *Circulation of Knowledge: Explorations in the History of Knowledge.* Lund: Nordic Academic Press, 2018.

Östling, Johan, Niklas Olsen, and David Larsson Heidenblad (eds.), *Histories of Knowledge in Postwar Scandinavia: Actors, Arenas, and Aspirations.* London: Routledge, 2020.

Paul, Herman J. (ed.), *How to Be a Historian: Scholarly Personae in Historical Studies, 1800–2000.* Manchester: Manchester University Press, 2019.

Pellandini-Simányi, Léna, 'The Financialization of Everyday Life', in Christian Borch, and Robert Wosnitzer (eds.), *The Routledge Handbook of Critical Finance Studies.* 2021, 278–99. https://library.oapen.org/handle/20.500.12657/41635.

Pietsch, Tamson, and Gabrielle Kemmis, 'The Careers of Humanities Students in Interwar Australia', *History of Humanities* 6:2 (2021), 617–34. https://doi.org/10.1086/715943.

Poole, Robert, *Earthrise: How Man First Saw the Earth*. New Haven: Yale University Press, 2008.

Preda, Alex, 'The Rise of the Popular Investor: Financial Knowledge and Investing in England and France, 1840–1880', *The Sociological Quarterly* 42:2 (2001), 205–32. https://doi.org/10.1111/j.1533-8525.2001.tb00031.x.

Proctor, Robert N., and Londa Schiebinger (eds.), *Agnotology: The Making and Unmaking of Ignorance*. Stanford: Stanford University Press, 2008.

Pyle, Cynthia M., 'Forum: Libraries as Laboratories for the Humanities. Introduction', *History of Humanities* 5:2 (2020), 467–85. https://doi.org/10.1086/710282.

Radkau, Joachim, *The Age of Ecology*. Cambridge: Polity Press, 2014.

Raj, Kapil, 'Beyond Postcolonialism ... and Postpositivism: Circulation and the Global History of Science', *Isis* 104:2 (2013), 337–47. https://doi.org/10.1086/670951.

Raj, Kapil, 'Go-Betweens, Travelers, and Cultural Translators', in Bernard Lightman (ed.), *A Companion to the History of Science*. Chichester: John Wiley, 2016, 39–56.

Raj, Kapil, *Relocating Modern Science: Circulation and the Construction of Knowledge in South Asia and Europe, 1650–1900*. Basingstoke: Palgrave Macmillan, 2007.

Renn, Jürgen, *The Evolution of Knowledge: Rethinking Science for the Anthropocene*. Princeton: Princeton University Press, 2020.

Ridder-Symoens, Hilde de (ed.), *A History of the University in Europe: Universities in Early Modern Europe (1500–1800)*. Cambridge: Cambridge University Press, 2003.

Roberts, Lissa, 'Situating Science in Global History: Local Exchanges and Networks of Circulation', *Itinerario* 33:1 (2009), 9–30. https://doi:10.1017/S0165115300002680.

Rome, Adam, *The Genius of Earth Day: How a 1970 Teach-In Unexpectedly Made the First Green Generation*. New York: Hill and Wang, 2013.

Rossiter, Margaret W., *Women Scientists in America before Affirmative Action, 1940–1972*. Baltimore: Johns Hopkins University Press, 1995.

Rüegg, Walter, and Hilde de Ridder-Symoens (eds.), *A History of the University in Europe: Universities in the Middle Ages*. Cambridge: Cambridge University Press, 1992.

Sarasin, Philipp, 'More Than Just Another Speciality: On the Prospects for the History of Knowledge', *Journal for the History of Knowledge* 1:1 (2020), 1–5. https://doi:10.5334/jhk.25.

Sarasin, Philipp, 'Was ist Wissensgeschichte?', *Internationales Archiv für Sozialgeschichte in der deutschen Literatur* 36:1 (2011), 159–72. https://doi:10.1515/iasl.2011.010.

Sarasin, Philipp, and Andreas Kilcher, 'Editorial. Nach Feierabend', in Philipp Sarasin, and Andreas Kilcher (eds.), *Zirkulationen: Zürcher Jahrbuch für Wissensgeschichte* 7 (2011), Zürich: Diaphanes Verlag, 7–11.

Schäfer, Dagmar, *The Crafting of the 10,000 Things: Knowledge and Technology in Seventeenth-Century China*. Chicago: University of Chicago Press, 2011.

Schildt, Axel, *Medien-Intellektuelle in der Bundesrepublik*. Göttingen: Wallstein, 2020.

Schildt, Axel, and Detlef Siegfried, *Deutsche Kulturgeschichte: Die Bundesrepublik – 1945 bis zur Gegenwart*. München: Hanser, 2009.

Schöttler, Peter (ed.), *Geschichtsschreibung als Legitimationswissenschaft: 1918–1945*. Frankfurt am Main: Suhrkamp, 1997.

Secord, James A., 'Inventing the Scientific Revolution', *Isis* 114:1 (2023), 50–76. https://doi:10.1086/723630.

Secord, James A., 'Knowledge in Transit', *Isis* 95:4 (2004), 654–72, https://doi:10.1086/430657.

Secord, James A., 'Project (2015): Knowledge in Transit', www.mpiwg-berlin.mpg.de/research/projects/knowledge-transit (accessed 6 March 2023).

Secord, James, *Visions of Science: Books and Readers at the Dawn of the Victorian Age*. Oxford: Oxford University Press, 2014.

Shapin, Steven, *The Scientific Revolution*. Chicago: Chicago University Press, 2018.

Slagstad, Rune, and Jan Messel (eds.), *Profesjonshistorier*. Oslo: Pax forlag, 2014.

Smith, Pamela H., *The Body of the Artisan: Art and Experience in the Scientific Revolution*. Chicago: University of Chicago Press, 2004.

Star, Susan Leigh, 'The Sociology of the Invisible: The Primacy of Work in the Writings of Anselm Strauss', in David R. Maines (ed.), *Social Organization and Social Process: Essays in Honor of Anselm Strauss*. Hawthorne: Aldine de Gruyter, 1991, 265–83.

Thue, Fredrik W., and Kim G. Helsvig, *Universitetet i Oslo 1811–2011: 1945–1975: Den store transformasjonen*. Oslo: Unipub, 2011.

Traflet, Janice, *A Nation of Small Shareholders: Marketing Wall Street after World War II*. Baltimore: Johns Hopkins University Press, 2013.

Verburgt, Lukas, and Peter Burke, 'Introduction: Histories of Ignorance', *Journal for the History of Knowledge* 2:1 (2021), 1–9. http://doi:10.5334/jhk.45

Vogt, William, *Road to Survival*. New York: W. Sloane Associates, 1948.

Wang, Sixiang, 'Chosŏn's Office of Interpreters: The Apt Response and the Knowledge Culture of Diplomacy', *Journal for the History of Knowledge* 1:1 (2020), 1–15. https://doi:10.5334/jhk.45.

Warde, Paul, Libby Robin, and Sverker Sörlin, *The Environment: A History of the Idea*. Baltimore: Johns Hopkins University Press, 2018.

Weber [Brilkman], Kajsa, 'The Circulation of Knowledge in Translations and Compilations', in Johan Östling, Erling Sandmo, David Larsson Heidenblad, Anna Nilsson Hammar, and Kari H. Nordberg (eds.), *Circulation of Knowledge: Explorations in the History of Knowledge*. Lund: Nordic Academic Press, 2018, 160–71.

Westberg, Johannes, 'Bright Nordic Lights: A Revitalised Interdisciplinary History of Education in the Massified Higher Education of the Nordics', *History of Education* 52:2–3 (2023), 1–25. https://doi:10.1080/0046760X.2022.2127003.

Westberg, Johannes, 'Knowledge Brokers beyond the Classroom: Nineteenth Century Teachers as Multifaceted Historical Actors', in Johan Östling, David Larsson Heidenblad, and Anna Nilsson Hammar (eds.), *Knowledge Actors: Revisiting Agency in the History of Knowledge*. Lund: Nordic Academic Press, 2023, 45–66.

Zloch, Stephanie, *Das Wissen der Einwanderungsgesellschaft: Deutschland von 1945 bis zur Schwelle des 21. Jahrhunderts*. Göttingen: Wallstein Verlag, 2023.

Acknowledgements

We wish to offer our heartfelt thanks to all those who have made this Element possible. The Element emerged from the dynamic environment at the Lund Centre for the History of Knowledge (LUCK) at Lund University. We are especially grateful to our colleagues Anna Nilsson Hammar and Martin Ericsson for having read the manuscript in its entirety and offered valuable comments. Erik Bodensten, Isak Hammar, Evelina Kallträsk, Björn Lundberg, and Kajsa Weber also provided us with helpful perspectives. The same goes for the group of Master's students – Olof Bärtås, Maria Carlsson, Asger Wienberg, and Emma Wildt – who read the manuscript version of the text. From outside our own department Magnus Linnarsson (Stockholm) and Frans Lundgren (Uppsala) have contributed constructive criticism. In addition, two anonymous peer reviewers have scrutinised our text and made many useful comments. We are also grateful for the continuing dialogue with Fredrik Thue and his colleagues at the Centre for the Study of Professions at Oslo Metropolitan University. More generally, we have also drawn a great deal of inspiration from all the stimulating exchanges with scholars in the growing global community of historians of knowledge. Lena Olsson has translated the text from Swedish into English with precision and commitment. Our financiers, mainly the Knut and Alice Wallenberg Foundation, Riksbankens Jubileumsfond, and the Crafoord Foundation, have made it economically possible for us to work on this book. Last but not least, we wish to thank Daniel Woolf, who first offered us the opportunity to write an Element in this series and then with a great measure of sympathy and professionalism guided us through the whole process.

Cambridge Elements $\equiv$

Historical Theory and Practice

Elements in the Series

The Theory and Philosophy of History: Global Variations
João Ohara

The Transformation of History in the Digital Age
Ian Milligan

Historians' Virtues: From Antiquity to the Twenty-First Century
Herman Paul

Confronting Evil in History
Daniel Little

Progress and the Scale of History
Tyson Retz

*Collaborative Historical Research in the Age of Big Data: Lessons
from an Interdisciplinary Project*
Ruth Ahnert, Emma Griffin, Mia Ridge and Giorgia Tolfo

A History of Big History
Ian Hesketh

Archaeology as History: Telling Stories from a Fragmented Past
Catherine J. Frieman

The Fabric of Historical Time
Zoltán Boldizsár Simon and Marek Tamm

Writing the History of Global Slavery
Trevor Burnard

Plural Pasts: Historiography between Events and Structures
Arthur Alfaix Assis

The History of Knowledge
Johan Östling and David Larsson Heidenblad

A full series listing is available at: www.cambridge.org/EHTP

Printed in the United States
by Baker & Taylor Publisher Services